# Sports in World History

Why are human beings athletes? How did the sports we know today develop in the world?

Modern sports emerged from a background of traditional sports in the nineteenth and early twentieth centuries. These sports were a product of the industrial revolution, the scientific revolution and urbanization. This lively and clear survey provides a wide-ranging overview of the history of modern sports, covering such topics as:

- How the major modern sports came about and how they spread throughout the world with the help of enthusiastic individuals, sports organizations, the YMCA and the Olympic movement
- Discussions of some of the most popular modern world sports including: soccer, basketball, baseball, cricket, table tennis, tennis, formula one racing, golf, swimming, skiing, volleyball, track and field, boxing, judo and cycling. These are among the most popular, although there are some 300 sports in the world
- The history of both Western and non-Western sports in depth, as well as the increasing globalization of sports today
- The challenges facing the world of sports today, such as commercialization and the use of performance-enhancing drugs

**David G. McComb** is Emeritus Professor of History at Colorado State University, where he taught courses in world history and sports history. He is the author of *Sports: An Illustrated History* (1999).

## Themes in World History
Series editor: Peter N. Stearns

The *Themes in World History* series offers focused treatment of a range of human experiences and institutions in the world history context. The purpose is to provide serious, if brief, discussions of important topics as additions to textbook coverage and document collections. The treatments will allow students to probe particular facets of the human story in greater depth than textbook coverage allows, and to gain a fuller sense of historians' analytical methods and debates in the process. Each topic is handled over time – allowing discussions of changes and continuities. Each topic is assessed in terms of a range of different societies and religions – allowing comparisons of relevant similarities and differences. Each book in the series helps readers deal with world history in action, evaluating global contexts as they work through some of the key components of human society and human life.

**Gender in World History**
Peter N. Stearns

**Consumerism in World History: The Global Transformation of Desire**
Peter N. Stearns

**Warfare in World History**
Michael S. Neiberg

**Disease and Medicine in World History**
Sheldon Watts

**Western Civilization in World History**
Peter N. Stearns

**The Indian Ocean in World History**
Milo Kearney

**Asian Democracy in World History**
Alan T. Wood

**Revolutions in World History**
Michael D. Richards

**Migration in World History**
Patrick Manning

**Sports in World History**
David G. McComb

**The United States in World History**
Edward J. Davies II

# Sports in World History

David G. McComb

Routledge
Taylor & Francis Group

NEW YORK AND LONDON

First published 2004
by Taylor & Francis Inc.
270 Madison Ave, New York, NY 10016

Simultaneously published in the UK
by Routledge
2 Milton Park, Park Square, Abingdon,
Oxon OX14 4RN

*Routledge is an imprint of the Taylor & Francis Group*

Typeset in Garamond and Gill Sans by
Keystroke, Jacaranda Lodge, Wolverhampton
Printed and bound in Great Britain by
MPG Books Ltd, Bodmin

*British Library Cataloguing in Publication Data*
A catalogue record for this book is available from the British Library

*Library of Congress Cataloging in Publication Data*
McComb, David G.
   Sports in world history / by David G. McComb.
      p. cm. — (Themes in world history)
   Includes bibliographical references and index.
   1. Sports—History. 2. World history. I. Title. II. Series.
   GV571.M37 2004
   796′.09—dc22                                        2004003808

ISBN 0–415–31811–4 (hbk)
ISBN 0–415–31812–2 (pbk)

# Contents

# Preface

Upon meeting someone for the first time at a social gathering one of the initial questions asked is, "What do you do?" The question is an attempt to establish some sort of identification, or connection, or perhaps a pecking order. It refers to economic work. In the past 25 years when this has happened to me I have answered, "I teach at a university." The inevitable follow-up question then was, "Well, what do you teach?" I would answer, "I teach the history of sport," pause, and carefully observe the reaction. Almost always the response was either, "Um," revealing little interest, or "Oh!" showing surprise and enthusiasm. The course of the conversation was then determined.

Students, academics, professional people, or others, seem to be divided into those who possess an almost inborn interest in sports, and those who don't. Either sports are seen as trivial and insignificant, or they are looked upon with curiosity and attention. People often read the sports pages of a newspaper and watch sporting events on television without ever thinking about their interest. They just enjoy the experience. They are the ones who say "Oh!", and this book is written for them.

# Chapter 1

# Introduction

It took a while for scholars in the twentieth century to recognize the significance of sports. Philosophers, sociologists, anthropologists, and physical educators preceded historians into the sports field, but enthusiasts established the North American Society for Sport History complete with a journal in 1973. In 30 years the small academic group has grown from 163 members to 380. Scattered through colleges and universities in North America, Europe, and Australia now are courses about sports, and although sports history is still a subtopic it is accepted in course curriculums and as a subject for serious research. It is no longer viewed as a boondoggle for instructors who wish to deduct the cost of stadium tickets from their income tax.

## What is sport?

Strangely enough, there has been a problem about defining the word "sport." Everyone knows what it means, and yet there is confusion. For instance, are fishing, hunting, skiing, or hiking sports? Most would agree that these activities are a kind of recreation, and a sort of sport. What happens, however, when there is a sponsored contest to catch the largest bass, or to find out who can ski over a set of mountain moguls with the fastest time? Most would agree that these activities are still sports, but that there is a difference in the intensity or seriousness of the physical effort involved. In explanation, physical educators have suggested a continuum for sports with recreation, or play, at one end of the line and athletics at the other.

Recreation is mainly for fun, or exercise, or relaxation—such as a game of noontime basketball at a local athletic club. At the other end of the continuum with athletics there is a high degree of training, investment, and coaching, along with spectators, rules, publicity, and institutional control such as with a varsity basketball game at a university. The amount of sheer fun diminishes, and the amount of serious work increases as you move from recreation to athletics. But, all along the line there is a combination of physical prowess, rules, and competition—the main ingredients of sports. It is less so with recreation, more so with athletics. In this book I emphasize the history of athletics rather than recreation, and thus, incidentally, leave out recreational games such as chess, or bridge because they lack any significant degree of physical effort. Also, in most cases when I use the words "sports," or "contests," and sometimes "games" as in the instance of Olympic Games they are used as synonyms for "athletics."

## The problem of periodization

Another special problem for sports historians beyond uncovering when and why and where sports developed in the past has been the construction of some sort of framework, or theory, to analyze and compare sports at different times and places. Scholars working with world history probably have struggled with this problem more than others. Generally, for teaching purposes world historians have adopted the division of time used by those teaching Western Civilization—ancient, medieval, and modern with the modern period beginning at 1500 CE. Still, there is much debate about periodization, particularly among world systems advocates who select the thirteenth, sixteenth, or eighteenth centuries as the most important era for trade and commerce. In contrast, for the development and spread of modern sports the nineteenth and twentieth centuries are the most important.

This is the time period when modern sports evolved and achieved a global distribution through the purposeful action of soldiers, imperial administrators, Christian missionaries, sports organizations, devotees, and businessmen. Traditional sports, those played by indigenous peoples, for the most part, rarely developed a global span. The sports that became global were those carried by the Europeans and Americans who reached into the world as a part of their historical evolution, communication, and influence. Thus, recent sports history fits roughly into the structure of modernization theory.

## Modernization theory

This idea argues that as a result of the industrial and scientific revolutions, urbanization, and the growth of capitalism the Western European nations and the United States developed into wealthy modern states that emphasized rationality, standardization, uniformity, order, material progress, bureaucratic government, and corporate control. The resulting increase in leisure and income for people in such a circumstance made possible the commercialization and professional development of spectator sports as pastimes. Modern states thus escaped the static, tradition bound, economically poor, ritualistic, hierarchical conditions of the pre-modern world.

Critics of modernization theory have pointed out its Western bias, the impersonal driving forces, the lack of power to predict non-Western developments, and an absence of consideration for traditional values or internal motivations. Also, critics have been impelled by a fear that modernization means cultural imperialism and globalization which leads, in turn, to a homogenized world culture. In regard to world sports there is some truth in this. Common rules for soccer and basketball, for example, are used world wide, and the conventions for the sports came from the West. Still the fear of homogenization or Eurocentrism does not decrease the power of the theory.

Although not well developed and somewhat misused, as historian Peter Stearns has pointed out, modernization theory serves as a useful tool for understanding the relationships of major forces in history such as the industrial revolution. Modernization theory, indeed, has been helpful in world comparative studies, business history, and sports history. Allen Guttmann, an American Studies professor at Amherst College, used it to explicate the differences between traditional and modern sport. For Guttmann the modern period really was different, and most sports historians agree with him. Time, however, does not rest and at the present there is speculation that sports may have entered into a postmodern period.

## Postmodernism

Starting in the 1960s architects, artists, and actors broke through the boundaries of modernism. They mixed styles, challenged orthodoxy, and abandoned accepted rules of conduct or taste. For example, architect Philip Johnson playfully placed a Chippendale-like pediment atop the AT&T Building completed in New York in 1984. Startled critics said it made the skyscraper look like a grandfather clock rather than a straight-lined, rectangular modern office building. Another example, Barnett Newman's radical, welded, rusted steel sculpture, *The Broken Obelisk*, symbolic of the interrupted life of Martin Luther King, Jr, became a part of the Rothko Chapel in Houston, Texas in 1971. It was recognized as a great piece of art, but it was not based upon the realism of nature. Theme parks, such as those provided by the Disney Corporation replaced reality with amusing simulations. As a part of the opening act of the 2003 MTV awards show pop star Madonna shocked the audience by passionately kissing her two fellow female singers, Britney Spears and Christina Aguilera. This act crossed a boundary involving relationships between sexes and caused a ripple of comments.

In sports too there occurred a breaking of boundaries. For example, in

1965 Judge Roy Hofheinz opened the Astrodome, the first air-conditioned sports stadium large enough to enclose a baseball field. Critics and players both hated and praised it, and the Astrodome began a trend toward the construction of large enclosed athletic fields, something never done before. Amateur rules of competition broke down under the weight of the Cold War, and television with an emphasis upon entertainment blurred and changed sports rules. Television executives forced the timing of athletic contests such as those of golf, American football, and tennis to meet a broadcast format. Extreme sports, those outside the normal limits such as skateboarding and surfing competition, appeared in the 1990s. After lamenting the decline of "first-class cricket" forced by the needs of television, Australian historians Bob Stewart and Aaron Smith concluded, "Spectacular, entertaining, novel, and time-compressed contests are the defining characteristics of postmodern sport."

Neither modernism, nor postmodernism, however, constitutes an accepted monolithic theory. Nonetheless, it seems that the characteristics of sports at the current moment are somewhat different than those of modern sports delimited by Allen Guttmann. More time, of course, will be needed for historians with their 20–20 hindsight to clarify these changes and suppositions. Analysis based upon modernization theory and postmodern speculations, however, illuminates the place of sports in human society.

## Sports and culture

Sporting activities are a cultural phenomenon and thus a part of the larger society of which they are a part. It is a common cliché that sports reveal the values of a society as illustrated by the often quoted declaration of American intellectual Jacques Barzun in 1954, "Whoever wants to know the heart and mind of America had better learn baseball, the rules and realities of the game—and do it by watching first some high school or small town teams."

Sports are an expression, or a statement, by a society about its interests, history, and character. Economics, politics, technology, religion, social issues such as gender or race, geography, and ethics can be observed in the rules and realities of sports. Shifts in these conditions influence sporting activities. Baseball, for example, is no longer the great American pastime. As sports sociologist D. Stanley Eitzen observed about America, "Baseball, then, represents what we were—an inner-directed, rural, individualistic society. It continues to be popular because of our longing for the peaceful past. Football, on the other hand, is popular now because it symbolizes what we now are—an other-directed, urban-technical, corporate-bureaucratic society." Sports, consequently, are similar to other cultural expressions such as sculpture, painting, music, dance, theater, motion pictures, and literature.

As society moves into a postmodern era, then sports too will become a part of the drift, and, at times, become a cultural leader. That is to be expected.

## Sports as art

It is helpful to think of sports as an art form—as a performing art. Sports share with other cultural expressions an appeal to the emotions, aesthetics, drama, entertainment, and inspiration. The athlete can be considered an artist with a certain amount of self-expression and spontaneity. The athlete must play within rules, of course, but so must a musician or actor. Compared to other arts the sports venues are different, an athlete's use of prohibited drugs may be a factor, and the outcome of a sporting event is always uncertain. An unsure outcome is not the case with plays or musical compositions where the musician or actor must follow what is written. The athlete may be closer to a jazz player or a writer where the opportunity to improvise is greater. Sports constitute a different sort of art form to be sure, but an art form nonetheless.

As a cultural expression, like painting or music or theater, sports might be considered unnecessary for human existence. For instance, although sports can inflame the emotions sporting events do not cause wars. They do not end wars, nor is there any good evidence that sporting comradeship will prevent wars. After all, there have been two world wars, a cold war, and numerous regional conflicts during the era of the modern Olympic Games. Sports, moreover, do not drive the economies of the world, nor determine foreign policy. In the grand expanse of the cosmos there is no indication that the result of a football game really means anything at all. Does God care which side wins? Are the Chicago Cubs and Boston Red Sox baseball teams really cursed? Who can tell?

As with other cultural programs in the schools there is no quantifiable evidence that sports are necessary for students. There is much anecdotal testimony, however, of the usefulness of the arts, including sports, for creating multidimensional, or well-rounded, lively individuals. People in all times and places have invented cultural institutions because they enrich the quality of life. Athletic events for both spectators and participants prompt conversations that cut through all divisions of society, and sports metaphors sprinkle the language—"a level playing field," "a sticky wicket," "on target," "throw in the towel." As sociologist Garry J. Smith commented, "Favorite teams, favorite players and a knowledge of sports lore all provide grist for conversation."

Physical contests, moreover, are probably as old as humankind. Anthropologist Robert R. Sands looks upon sport as a "cultural universal," a human constant that invites cross-cultural comparisons and provides a "blueprint of those important and valued behaviors that are the foundation of the larger culture in which sport is embedded." Like other cultural representations sports are an art form that help to measure what it means to be a human being.

## The organization of the book

In Chapter 2 I take a look at the basic motives, or reasons, involved in the creation of sports. I use mixed examples but many from pre-modern times to illustrate the reasons and to provide a demonstration about the rich history of sport before 1800. One of the virtues of world history is to make comparisons across time and space in order to elicit differences and similarities, and this chapter offers that opportunity. The main thrust of the book, however, is to follow the history of modern international sports. Chapter 3 traces the beginnings of modern athletics, and Chapter 4 tracks the spread of these activities around the world. The final chapter discusses the importance of the globalization of modern sports.

The emphasis is upon the major world sports, roughly the top ten, as measured by the interest of fans and participants. All sports cannot be covered, but unanswered questions about other activities probably can be satisfied by reference to the *Encyclopedia of World Sport* (1996) that provides descriptions of 300 sports around the globe. At times I have given the basic rules of a sport, but they are partial at best. For greater detail about rules a reader can consult the *Rand McNally Illustrated Dictionary of Sports* (1978), *Rules of the Game* (1990), or *Sports, the Complete Visual Reference* (2000). For statistical information the annual almanacs by *Sports Illustrated* or *ESPN* are useful.

## Further reading

Melvin L. Adelman, "Modernization Theory and Its Critics," *Encyclopedia of American Social History* (New York: Scribners, 1993), vol. I, pp. 348–56; Gerry Brown and Michael Morrison (eds), *ESPN: Information Please Sports Almanac* (New York: Hyperion, 2002). Diagram Group, *Rules of the Game* (New York: St. Martin's Press, 1990); Editors of Sports Illustrated, *Sports Almanac* (Boston: Little Brown and Company, 1996); Francois Fortin, *Sports: the Complete Visual Reference* (Willowdale, Ontario, Canada: Firefly Books, 2000); Allen Guttmann, *From Ritual to Record: The Nature of Modern Sports* (New York: Columbia University Press, 1978); David Levinson and Karen Christensen (eds), *Encyclopedia of World Sport* (Santa Barbara, California: ABC-CLIO, 1996) 3 vols; Benjamin Lowe, *The Beauty of Sport* (Englewood Cliffs, New Jersey: Prentice-Hall, 1977); Robert R. Sands, *Anthropology, Sport, and Culture* (Westport, CT: Bergin & Garvey, 1999); Garry J. Smith, "The Noble Sports Fan," in D. Stanley Eitzen (ed.), *Sport in Contemporary Society: An*

*Anthology* (New York: St. Martin's, 1993, fourth edition), pp. 3–14; Peter N. Stearns, "Modernization and Social History: Some Suggestions and a Muted Cheer," *Journal of Social History*, vol. 14 (Winter 1980), pp. 189–209; Bob Stewart and Aaron Smith, "Australian Sport in a Postmodern Age," *International Journal of the History of Sport*, vol. 17 (June–September 2000), pp. 278–304; Graeme Wright, *Rand McNally Illustrated Dictionary of Sports* (Chicago: Rand McNally & Company, 1978).

# Chapter 2

# The Athletic Imperative and the Reasons for Sport

Every person is born with athletic capability and every person is predestined, "hard wired," to develop that physical potential. This is an imperative that is a part of human nature. The first part of this chapter explores that foundational aspect of sports and then in the second part offers a taxonomy of influences, or reasons, involved in the formation of sports.

*[handwritten margin note: All we athletically capable, pre-destined to develop that ability]*

## The athletic imperative

Abraham Maslow (1908–1970) who was the foremost twentieth-century theorist concerning human motivation recognized the fact of predestined physicality. He was one of the three great psychologists of the twentieth century. Observations of his own child led him away from the other two great theorists of psychology, Sigmund Freud (1856–1939), who examined repressed thoughts, and B. F. Skinner (1904–1990), who studied the influence of outside forces on behavior. Maslow noticed that his baby had an inner agenda and timetable that instructed the child to roll over, to walk, and to move independent of his parent's teaching. Maslow and other scholars realized that physical activity was inborn to human beings and was a major force in human evolution. In growing up children learn to walk, throw, run, climb, carry, lift and perform basic motor skills. Developing these skills and using them throughout life is common to all humankind. In short, humans are sentient beings impelled to move; it is the biologic destiny of the species. Thus, all humans begin life with the potential to be an athlete.

*[handwritten margin note: the FACT of predestined capability]*

*[handwritten margin note: Humans inherently need to move through space]*

It would appear, in addition, that there exists for humans a certain joy in movement. The great runner Roger Bannister who grew up awkward and introspective in Bath, England recalled a moment of physical revelation while on a beach during his youth:

> In this supreme moment I leapt in sheer joy. I was startled, and frightened by the tremendous excitement that so few steps could create.

I glanced round uneasily to see if anyone was watching. A few more steps—self-consciously now and firmly gripping the original excitement. The earth seemed almost to move with me. I was running now, and a fresh rhythm entered my body. No longer conscious of my movement I discovered a new unity with nature. I had found a new source of power and beauty, a source I never dreamt existed.

Maslow theorized about a "hierarchy of needs" that would lead individuals forward to self-actualization and peak experiences of elation and intense awareness. Psychologists speak, now, of these moments as "flow" experiences when time stands still and concentration is complete. For athletes these are instances when everything "works," when they are "hot," when they are in harmony with the demands of their sport. John Jerome, author of a book about biomechanics, calls it a "sweet spot," and remembers nostalgically a moment from his youth while throwing rocks at bottles. "Mostly I recall the haunting power I felt on that occasional throw when I knew as the stone left my hand that it was going to hit its target."

During the final lap of his historic effort in 1954 that broke the four-minute barrier of the mile run Roger Bannister remembered:

I had a moment of mixed joy and anguish, when my mind took over. It raced well ahead of my body and drew my body compellingly forward. I felt that the moment of a lifetime had come. There was no pain, only a great unity of movement and aim. The world seemed to stand still, or did not exist. The only reality was the next two hundred yards of track under my feet.

George Sheehan, the late medical editor of *Runner's World Magazine* and jogger's guru, quoted a world-class surfer, Michael Hynson, who said, "When you become united with a wave, you lose your identity on one level and make contact with it again on a higher plane." About his own "runner's high" Sheehan commented,

My feelings span the spectrum from simple sensual pleasure to joy, from contentment to a peace beyond understanding. The simplest way to describe these varying phenomena is to say they are peak experiences. Each is a state of being lost in the present, of becoming timeless, selfless, outside of space, history, and anxiety. Maslow said this state was a diluted, more secular, and more frequent version of the mystical experience.

There exists little scientific data to support the existence of a "joy of movement" or "peak experiences," mainly just observation and anecdotal commentary. Yet, these aspects of human life seem to be the wellspring for sports. They are universal and are fundamental for the pleasure and wonder that sports provide. Anyone who has been a dedicated athlete likely will have had personal awareness of these feelings and will be able to recognize them in others.

## The role of competition

Another basic element for athletes involves competition, a way to measure physical skills, and an incentive to inspire the best efforts. As Benjamin Lowe expressed it in *The Beauty of Sport* (1977), "Competition is the whetstone against which the athlete sharpens his abilities in his search for excellence," and such rivalry appears in our earliest history. For example, while on a recent research trip to Zimbabwe, zoologist Bernd Heinrich looked under a rock overhang and discovered an ancient pictograph showing a line of small sticklike human figures, carrying bows and arrows, and running in full stride. The leader at the far right had his arms thrown upward in the athlete's universal gesture of triumph at the end of a race. Heinrich, an amateur marathon runner, concluded:

> This involuntary gesture is reflexive for most runners who have fought hard, who have breathed the heat and smelled the fire, and then felt the exhilaration of triumph over adversity. The image of the Bushmen remains for me an iconic reminder that the roots of our running, our competitiveness, and our striving for excellence go back very far and very deep.

References to athletic competition sprinkle ancient literature and folklore. In the world's oldest piece of literature, *The Epic of Gilgamesh*, which originates in Babylonia about 2300 BCE, Gilgamesh, the hero of the story, meets Enkidu who challenges his superiority with a wrestling match. "The two grappled in combat, and struggled and lowed and roared like two wild bulls," says the poem. "They destroyed the pillar of the door and the wall shook. . . . But when Gilgamesh, bracing his foot on the floor, bent over and threw Enkidu, the heat of his fury cooled and he turned away to leave." Enkidu then acknowledged the loss and after this competition the two became the best of friends and companions for life. Although the story is contained in an epic poem of folkloric origin, interestingly, the Babylonian calendar designated "Gilgamesh's month" as a time for wrestling competitions.

In ancient Egypt to prove their prowess pharaohs hunted and competed with soldiers. A stele from Giza recorded the accomplishments of Amenophis II (1438–12 BCE):

Nor was there anyone who could bend a bow like him, and no one excelled him in running against others. His arms were so strong that he was never faint when he grasped the oar and rowed abaft his arrow-swift ship, the best of the crew of two hundred.

We still prefer leaders who are physically fit and political candidates will go out of the way to release medical exams or photographs of themselves while jogging, sailing, or playing golf, softball, or some amateur sport. Of course in this instance of Amenophis II, who would have the temerity to beat a pharaoh in a sporting contest, or openly doubt the truth of a legend about an Egyptian prince who won the love of a lady and defeated other suitors by jumping 37 meters straight up the wall of a tower to her window?

Perhaps the most interesting tale of athletic competition and love, however, involves the supposed beginning of chariot racing in ancient Greece. Oinomaos, a Greek king, had a beautiful daughter of marriage-able age named Hippodameia. It was agreed that suitors would try to drive away with her in a chariot, and that the king would pursue the couple with his own swift horses and chariot. If caught, the king would kill the young man with a spear. When Pelops arrived to try his luck he noted 12 heads of previous contestants nailed to the palace gateway. Shrewd Pelops, however, bribed the king's charioteer, Myrtilos, with the promise of a lustful night in the arms of Hippodameia. Myrtilos, in return, replaced the bronze axle-pins of the king's chariot with beeswax.

Pelops then swept up the willing Hippodameia and raced off. The king pursued, but his chariot fell apart and he died when thrown to the ground. Instead of keeping his promise, however, Pelops cast Myrtilos off a cliff into the sea where, cursing the perfidy of Pelops, the charioteer drowned. For Greeks it was not necessary for a mythic hero to be virtuous, only cunning, and at the sacred grove of the Olympic Games they honored a burial mound as a shrine to Pelops and the origin of chariot racing. In the same place Hippodameia established the Heraia that honored Hera, the wife of the god Zeus, with athletic contests for girls.

Homer told the bloodiest tale of love and athletic competition at the conclusion of *The Odyssey* (760 BCE). When Odysseus returned home from the Trojan War after an absence of ten years he found the neighboring Greek men in an archery contest to see who would take over his lands and wife. Penelope, the loyal wife who had been told that Odysseus was dead, had agreed that she would wed any man who could string her husband's bow and fire an arrow through "every socket hollow" of twelve iron axheads. None of the suitors could even bend the stout bow enough to hook the bowstring. But Odysseus disguised as a poor vagabond stepped up, strung the bow, plucked it so that the string sang with the "voice of a swallow," and shot an arrow through the axheads. He then drew other arrows and slaughtered the men who had invaded his house and tried to steal his wife and property.

In summary, the athletic imperative is a part of all people and a part of evolutionary history. Competition, if not inborn, is still of ancient lineage, important in the evolutionary process, and necessary for survival. As a well-known aphorism among contemporary runners states:

*Every morning in Africa, an antelope wakes up. It knows it must outrun the fastest lion, or it will be killed. Every morning in Africa, a lion wakes up. It knows it must run faster than the fastest antelope, or it will starve. It doesn't matter whether you're a lion or an antelope—when the sun comes up, you'd better be running.*

## Secondary influences

Through time there have been secondary influences that have provided shape and style to the athletic imperative—vocation, warfare, religion, entertainment, geography, and eros. In traditional sports, the spontaneous games of indigenous people, the various motives are so interwoven that individual threads of influence are difficult to pull out from the fabric of the activity. For analytical purposes, however, these secondary influences are set apart for comment along with examples. It is easy to argue even with these examples that there are frequently mixed reasons, and that often it is necessary to rely on prima facie evidence or common sense about the motives. Illustrations for comparison are taken from a variety of places and times mainly before 1800, after which the first modern sports become apparent. Even with such a time parameter, it should be understood that traditional sports have continued to emerge. Riding and competing with surfboards, mountain bikes, skateboards, and snowboards are examples.

## Vocation

The drawings of prehistoric runners observed by Bernd Heinrich in Zimbabwe were superimposed upon a hunting scene and the natives carried bows and arrows. Hunting was a necessary occupation and running was probably the first sport, an easy carry-over from hunting. Running required nothing in the way of equipment, just a will to race. Such races were a part of New Year festivals in Akkadian (2500 BCE) and Hittite civilizations (1200 BCE). Indeed, the first event recorded for the ancient Olympic Games in 776 BCE was a sprint, and it was the only event for the first 13 Olympiads. The length of the Greek stadium, a *stade*, was about 200 meters which is the distance that a human being can run at an all-out sprint. Over time the Greeks added other races, as long as 20–24 lengths of the stadium.

The most famous current long distance race, the marathon, has a vocational background. It was never an event of the ancient Olympics, and has a root in the story of Pheidippides, a professional courier who ran with messages from one place to another through the Greek countryside. The historical basis for his story is shaky with only a brief mention by the historian Herodotus (485–425 BCE) about a messenger and a comment by the biographer Plutarch (46–120) some 500 years later.

According to the legend, when the invading Persians landed near the city-state of Athens in 490 BCE the Athenians sent Pheidippides to their sister city-state of Sparta to ask for help. The Spartans refused for the moment because of religious reasons, and Pheidippides ran home with the bad news. The Athenians then launched a successful surprise attack against the Persians and sent Pheidippides, who had participated in the battle, home with the news of victory. The courier then ran the 26 miles or so back to the agora of Athens where he pronounced, "Rejoice, we conquer!" Having run 350 miles over hilly trails in five days Pheidippides then dropped dead. Although details of the story are doubtful, the idea of the modern marathon, the run from the battlefield of Marathon to Athens, was born and became a part of the modern Olympic Games that began in 1896.

Also of interest is the running race on the beach at the funeral games of Patroclus described by Homer in the *Iliad* (760 BCE). This segment of the book contains the best description of ancient Greek athletics, but a reader must remember that gods and goddesses played an active role in Greek life. Odysseus, one of the contestants, was running a close second and prayed as he neared the finish line, "Hear me goddess. I need your valuable aid. Come down and speed my feet." Athena heard his prayer, gave him a second wind, and tripped the leading runner so that he slid face down, mouth open through a pile of cow dung. Odysseus won the race and his opponent spitting out manure exclaimed, "Damnation take it! I swear it was the goddess tripped me up—the one who always dances attendance, like a mother, on Odysseus." Athena who carried the shield and spear of her father Zeus, was the Greek goddess of warfare and victory.

When successful hunting depended upon the accurate use of hunting tools—bows, arrows, spears, and later guns—target shooting was a natural result. Evidence of archery can be found almost everywhere in the world including in the prehistoric cave paintings of Spain and France. Archaeologist Howard Carter (1873–1939) found bows and arrows in the tomb of Pharaoh Tutankhamen (1348–1340 BCE); the temple wall at Nineveh portrayed King Asshurbanipal (669–640 BCE) with a bow and arrow killing lions released from cages. At the funeral games of Patroclus Achilles held an archery contest to see who could hit a pigeon tied to the top of a ship's mast erected on the beach. The first contestant's arrow cut the cord that held the pigeon, but the winner hit the bird high overhead in mid-flight.

In China proficiency with a bow and arrow became a part of the state civil service exams during the Tang Dynasty (618–906), and in Japan archery contests both standing and on horseback became important for court ceremonies in the seventh century. In Medieval Europe archers shot at various targets including the popinjay, a wooden bird placed on a high pole, and stories about archers abounded in folklore. The legendary bowman Robin Hood, subject of almost 40 English and Scottish ballads, supposedly lived in Sherwood Forest of England near Nottingham where he robbed the rich and gave to the poor. The legendary William Tell of Switzerland shot an apple off the head of his son with an arrow and became a symbol of resistance to oppression in the early fourteenth century.

Archery, however, became more of a pastime after the invention of guns, and on the American frontier, contests with rifles replaced bows and arrows. John James Audubon (1785–1851) the great bird artist, described backwoods rifle competitions that required driving nails with a bullet and "barking" a squirrel. The shooter hit the bark near a squirrel so that the concussion, not the bullet, killed it. Farther to the west in the 1820s and 1830s at an annual rendezvous the Rocky Mountain fur trappers exchanged their yearly catch of pelts for supplies and enjoyed a week of drunkenness, gambling, whoring, and brawling with impromptu contests of horse racing, wrestling, and tomahawk throwing.

One of the more enduring frontier sports that evolved from a vocation, or business, however, was rodeo. In northern Mexico and the American Southwest Spanish settlers established cattle ranches in the seventeenth and eighteenth centuries. American cowboys in the nineteenth century learned to handle cattle from the Spanish *vaqueros* and adopted their equipment. The work required special skills of roping, branding, and herding cattle, and moreover, wild horses had to be broken for ranch work. When cowboys met in a social setting, particularly in town on the July 4 holiday, it was natural for them to test their skills. Prescott, Arizona recorded an early rodeo in 1864 two years after the start of the town. Professional rodeo developed in the 1880s and William F. Cody popularized the sport with his wild-west shows that started in 1882.

## Warfare

It was an easy step to use the tools of hunting—bows and arrows, spears, horses, guns—to hunt and kill fellow human beings. In the ancient Olympic Games javelin throwing as a sport seems most closely related since the javelin was an offensive weapon used by soldiers from the Mycenaean age through the Roman Empire. It was hurled from a distance at an enemy before soldiers closed for hand-to-hand combat. Javelin throwing became an event at the Olympic Games as a part of the pentathlon—running, jumping, discus throwing, javelin throwing, and wrestling—in 708 BCE. The Greeks included boxing in 688 BCE; chariot racing in 680 BCE; horseback racing and the *pankration*, a combination of wrestling and boxing, in 648 BCE. In 520 BCE they added a short running race of men carrying armor—helmet, greaves, and shield—as the concluding event of the festival. All of these events reinforced and reflected skills useful in combat.

Unarmed combat can be found worldwide, but the ancient Greeks refined wrestling. At their games the combatants faced off from either a standing position or on the ground. In order to win it was necessary to throw a person to the ground three times from the standing position, or if on the ground force an opponent to admit defeat. There were no time or weight limits. Tripping was allowed, but biting, gouging, and grabbing the genitals was forbidden. The first sports hero, Milo from Croton in southern Italy, won at wrestling six times at Olympia (once in the boys' division) and might be considered the first "jock." Stories have lingered about him since the sixth century BCE: he once ate an entire 4-year-old heifer that he had carried around the Olympic site; on a bet he drank nine liters of wine at one sitting; he could break a cord tied around his forehead by holding his breath and swelling the veins in his head. After his final defeat at his seventh Olympiad by an opponent who refused to close with him—Milo dropped from exhaustion—the spectators cheered the fallen champion and paraded him around the stadium on their shoulders.

There was a cautionary end to Milo's story, however, as recorded by Pausanias, a tourist from Lydia who visited Olympia in the second century. While walking the countryside Milo came upon a fallen, drying log into which a farmer had driven wedges in order to split it. With overweening pride in his strength Milo sought to finish the job by inserting his hands into the partly open split and pull the log apart. When he tried to do this the wedges fell out and the log snapped together upon his fingers. He was trapped and that night Milo was attacked and eaten by wolves. Homer had warned that people who glory in their strength perish by it, and the story supported a long-enduring notion that athletes who have strong bodies often have weak minds.

Wrestling was also a major sport with ancient Egyptians and tomb paintings dating from about 2050 BCE at Beni Hasan on the Nile River 200 miles south of Alexandria reveal 122 pairs of men and boys in various wrestling positions. Virtually all of the modern wrestling moves are shown, but it is also clear from the pictures that for Egyptians there were no holds barred. Local pre-modern wrestling matches for harvest celebrations and marriage rituals have been observed in Africa and for recreation in India and the British Isles, but one of the most curious variations of wrestling occurred in Asia with sumo wrestling.

The origins of sumo are obscure, but reach back into court entertainment, religious ritual, and warfare. The earliest use of the word "sumo," interestingly, refers to a match between women. According to a story, Emperor Yuryaku, who supposedly ruled in the fifth century became annoyed when a royal carpenter bragged that he never made a mistake. The emperor ordered several of his female attendants to strip to the waist and wrestle in view of the carpenter. The disturbed workman then resumed his work and made an error, whereupon the emperor ordered the execution of the carpenter. In the eighth century sumo matches which were won simply by throwing an opponent were used at ceremonies to symbolize state power, and in the twelfth century wrestling was used as a part of training for hand-to-hand combat. At times, sumo was performed as part of a ritual at Shinto shrines, particularly by women to bring rain during drought. In time sumo wrestling carrying remnants of Shinto rituals evolved into a modern sport characterized by huge, nearly naked men grappling each other in a 12-foot ring. It is an example of a traditional sport that underwent changes to remain viable in the modern world.

Other unarmed combat techniques came out of Asia—t'ai chi ch'uan and shaolin ch'uan—that eventually evolved into judo, karate, and taekwando. These, however, were personal defenses invented in the sixth century that became sport only in the modern era. Boxing, also used for unarmed combat, had a longer lineage that reached back at least to ancient Mesopotamia. Votive tablets dating from around 3000 BCE found by archeologists at the Sumerian city of Khafaje, for instance, reveal wrestlers and boxers. In the tombs of the eighteenth dynasty in Egypt (1570–1320 BCE) researchers found pictures of boxers, wrestlers, and stick fighters. A decorated drinking goblet from Crete in 1500 BCE shows a boxer wearing a war helmet and a glove standing triumphantly over a sprawled opponent whose feet are in the air. The famous fresco from the island of Thira showing two children boxing dates from the same period.

When the ancient Greeks added boxing to their Olympic Games they allowed no holding or wrestling. It was permissible to hit a fallen man. Since there were no rounds, the fight lasted until someone was defeated. At times, to end a contest before nightfall, the boxers would exchange undefended blows to see who would drop. The fighters aimed primarily at the head rather than the body, and wrapped their fists with leather cords. Achilles proposed a boxing match at the funeral games of Patroclus and Epius accepted the challenge with one of the earliest examples of "trash talk." "I'll tell you what I mean to do," said Epius. "I am going to tear the fellow's flesh to ribbons and smash his bones. I recommend him to have all his mourners standing by to take him off when I have done with him."

These declarations were at first accepted in silence and then Euryalus stood up and prepared to fight. Epius, however, was as good as his talk and hit Euryalus a blow that took out his legs and lifted him "like a fish leaping up from the weed-covered sands and falling back into the dark water." Euryalus' friends gathered round and carried him off on "trailing feet," senseless with a lolling head, and spitting blood. Epius won a "sturdy mule" as a prize.

The most brutal of the Greek unarmed combat fights, however, was the *pankration*. It was so popular and the prizes so large that it became the first of the ancient Greek sports to be taken over by professionals. It was a combination of wrestling and boxing and although biting and gouging were forbidden breaking bones was not. The men fought until one surrendered by lifting a forefinger in the air. Pausanias, the Lydian tourist, noted a pankrationist who specialized in breaking fingers and another who liked to twist a leg out of its socket. Pausanias also told about Arrachion who died during an Olympic bout in 564 BCE. During the contest his opponent wrapped his legs around Arrachion from the back while strangling him with his hands. Arrachion, however, caused surrender by dislocating his opponent's toe. Unfortunately, Arrachion died at the same time, so the judges crowned his corpse with the olive wreath of victory.

Similar was the "rough and tumble" fighting that flourished in the American frontier during the eighteenth and early nineteenth centuries. There were few rules—no weapons allowed—and the fighters, accompanied with cursing and oaths, gouged, butted, scratched, choked, kicked, dismembered, wrestled and boxed without interference until someone surrendered and gave up. The grandest accomplishment was to gouge out an eyeball and fighters sharpened and hardened their fingernails for that purpose. Stories of mass fights with eyeballs, ears, and noses littering the battleground established place names such as "Fighting Creek," and "Gouge Eye." Explanation for the brutality lies in the dangerous frontier life where fighting was a necessity of survival, and also in the class differences, lack of family life, and excessive pride in personal male honor when there was not much else to be proud about.

A ball game played by American Indians offers a further example of unarmed warfare and sports. George Catlin (1796–1872), a frontier artist, observed a Choctaw match in the 1830s. He said the Indians placed goals made of two 25-foot upright poles, six feet apart with a cross piece at the top, on each end of a 250-yard, open field. After expansive betting and an all night dance the game started in the morning with some 6–700 players using a yard-long stick with an oval, netted hoop at the end. The players, using a stick in each hand, tried to catch and throw a small ball through the goals without touching the ball. There was a great deal of running, leaping, yelping, stirring of dust, hits in the face and shins, and individual fistfights until 100 goals were scored. After that the winner claimed the bets, everyone took a drink of whiskey, and the Indians went home. French Jesuits in the seventeenth century named the game "lacrosse" supposedly because the stick reminded them of a bishop's crosier, or staff. Although there were elements of entertainment, gambling, and ceremony in the event, the Indians used it as a training and conditioning exercise. The Indian word for the game, "baggataway," translates as "little brother of war."

Technology improved armed combat, especially the bow and arrow as a weapon of war. The crossbow with a bow mounted at right angles to a stock proved deadly at short range during the first crusade at the end of the eleventh century. The dreaded Mongolian cavalry of Genghis Khan in the thirteenth century terrorized Eastern Europe and Asia with a short, composite bow designed for a man on horseback. In the fourteenth century the famous English longbow, standing as tall as a man and capable of launching a yard-long arrow with enough force to penetrate armor at 180 meters distance, devastated the French knights in battle at Crecy in 1346 and again at Agincourt in 1415. The longbow was so well designed that it remained a sporting bow into the 1930s.

The knights sharpened their fighting skills with tournaments and melees where they tried to knock each other off their warhorses with blunted weapons. Mock fights had long taken place, but they were dangerous. The tourney itself faded from popularity after Henry II of France (1519–1559) entered a joust to please his mistress. The tip of his opponent's lance penetrated his visor and went into his eye socket. Henry died a short time later. Contests with swords led later to the disciplined modern sport of fencing where the combatants wore facemasks and survived with no injury. In feudal Japan the mercenary samurai practiced their art of killing with harmless bamboo swords and their training exercise eventually became the sport of Kendo in the latter part of the nineteenth century. Such sword practice, however, was so associated with warfare that it was banned during the American occupation of Japan and not revived until the 1950s.

It would seem, consequently, that warfare along with hunting has been the most significant inspiration for traditional sport. Catholic theologian Michael Novak commented, "The human animal is a warlike animal; conflict is as near to the truth about human relations, even the most intimate, as any other feature. Sports dramatize conflict." Even today warrior behavior can be glimpsed lurking in the background of the controlled and constrained sports we cherish. Commentators use military metaphors in sports such as "throw a bomb," "charge," and "blitz." The sneaker company, Converse, marketed a shoe in 2003 called "Loaded Weapon."

Military commanders, in turn, have sensed merit in sports training for soldiers. The Duke of Wellington probably never said, "The battle of Waterloo was won on the playing fields of Eton," but it was a sentiment firmly believed. Similar words by General Douglas MacArthur are posted on the gymnasium at West Point, the school for United States army officers: "Upon the fields of friendly strife/Are sown the seeds/That, upon other fields, on other days/Will bear the fruits of victory." This warfare–sports connection reveals something very fundamental about human nature—the combative characteristic of the human species and the resultant long experience with war. Sports as a cultural artifact mirror this singularity. However, there were additional influences on sports.

## Religion

The painting of men and women with wasp-like waists leaping over the back of a wild bull at the palace of Knossos on Crete is a mystery. Wearing boots, loin cloths, and smiles the performers grasp the bull straight on by the horns and as the bull throws them upward the acrobats land on the back of the bull, and somersault to the ground. No one knows the meaning of this activity, but the bull arenas were located next to temples and bull games were a prominent part of Minoan religion and civilization (3000–1000 BCE). The acrobatic displays may well symbolize the supremacy of a goddess religion over an older belief in the primacy of the wild bull.

Of equal mystery are the ball games of Mesoamerican civilization (1400 BCE–1500 CE). Scattered across the Yucatan jungles of Mexico and Guatemala are the ruins of stone cities that are the result of Mayan culture (300–900 CE). Interspersed in their temple complexes are numerous I-shaped ball courts of varying size. The Indians played a game in which the object was to hit a heavy rubber ball through a vertical ring placed high on the walls at mid-court. Only the hips or thighs could strike the ball to put it through the goal.

Unfortunately, only documentary fragments remain to describe the details of this 1,000-year-old game that the Mayas inherited from earlier cultures. Ball games are mentioned in the creation myths of the Indians and in the Florentine Codex preserved by the Spanish in the sixteenth century. From this it can be learned that leaders used the game for gambling and entertainment, but there exists no rulebook. Details remain unknown, and there is a modern interpretation that the winners were sacrificed to the gods, not the losers, because the winners had proven that they were worthy. Another curiosity is that the ball courts have no room for spectators. These were not stadiums; only the ancient Greeks, Etruscans, and Romans built such athletic facilities in the pre-modern world of sports.

More clearly seen is the religious infusion in the ancient Olympic Games of the Greeks. The games were dedicated to Zeus, the most powerful of their gods, and the Temple of Zeus at Olympia contained a seated 13-meter statue of the god made of gold, ebony, precious stones, and ivory. He supported

Nike, the winged harbinger of victory, in the open palm of his hand. The statue was considered to be one of the seven wonders of the ancient world, and offerings, prayers, and the awarding of the olive wreath of victory took place there. The site of Olympia, moreover, was located at the sacred grove of Demeter, the goddess of fertility, and her priestess was the only female allowed to view the games. The Greeks built the Temple of Hera, wife of Zeus, on the grounds, but it is likely that sacrifices to Hera took place at times other than the Olympics, such as during the Heraia which was a time of games for girls.

Elsewhere, the Greeks honored their gods with festivals such as the Isthmian games at Corinth dedicated to the god Poseidon and the Pythian games at Delphi dedicated to Apollo. Athens, named for Athena, celebrated the Panathenaea, a local festival filled with musical competitions, torch relays, chariot racing, trireme races, and male beauty contests to honor the goddess. After their conquest of Greece the Romans absorbed the various Greek sports, but dedicated them to their own gods, such as chariot racing in honor of Jupiter. Ironically, it was another religion that brought the eventual end of the Olympic Games after 1,100 years. The Christian emperor Theodosius of Rome stopped the contests in 393 CE because he thought they were pagan.

The religion of Islam also discourages sports development. Muhammad (570–632), the founder of Islamic civilization, approved of running, wrestling, archery, horseback riding, spear play, swimming, and tumbling for military training or relaxation. They were not to take precedence over religious obligations, however, and school sports never became a part of the Islamic educational system. The holy month of Ramadan requires fasting with no food or water during daylight hours, a dictate of Islam still followed by 1.2 billion people. Such a disruption of nutrition would seemingly hurt an athlete, but Hakeem Olajuwon, a Nigerian Muslim who rigidly fasted and played professional basketball for the Houston Rockets said, "Religion is supposed to help you. It isn't supposed to take anything away. It enhances my game." During Ramadan in 1997 Olajuwon's average points per game rose by three points.

Islam also dictates against nakedness. Women are to be kept veiled and secluded, and men are not supposed to expose their knees. Of course there are variations between Islamic groups, but the power of the faith is remarkable. Runner Hassiba Boulmerka became the first Algerian to win a world championship in 1991, while she was denounced at home by Muslim clerics for "running with naked legs in front of men." Because of death threats, she trained in Italy, employed bodyguards, and carried a .38 caliber pistol. She won a gold medal for Algeria in the 1,500-meter run at the 1992 Olympics. Iranian women worked out for the 1996 kayak events while wearing the prescribed hooded robes designed to hide the female body.

It was difficult to compete while wearing such constricting garments and their coach admitted that the clothing added ten seconds over a 500-meter course. In 2000 the fundamentalist Islamic sect Taliban of Kandahar, Afghanistan, interrupted a soccer game with Pakistan and arrested twelve Pakistani players, also Muslim, for wearing shorts. The twelve players were sent home after the Taliban shaved their heads as punishment. In general, the Muslim world has been more concerned about religion than athletics and thus has contributed less to the ranks of world champions and to the history of sport.

Christianity, another world religion, over time has both supported and condemned sporting activity. During the Middle Ages in Europe various ball games similar to bowling and soccer were played on holidays, often on church grounds. French monks played a game of hitting a small ball over a rope strung across a cloister. Progressing from hitting with an open hand, to a webbed glove, to a paddle marked the beginning of tennis and paddle games. The Italians, meanwhile, scheduled horse races on their Saint's days.

After the Protestant Reformation during the Puritan upheaval of the seventeenth century in England, however, the Puritan magistrates suppressed recreation of all sorts unless for the glory of God. They thought that sports were frivolous and that idleness was a sin. Puritan settlers in the New England area of what later became the United States carried the repressive ideas across the Atlantic Ocean. Weekdays were meant for work and Sundays for all-day worship. Transgressors were fined and punished. In the early history of the Plymouth colony on Christmas Day, 1621, for example, a newly arrived group played stool ball (an early bat and ball game) and threw cabers in the street. The outraged governor of the colony forced them to stop and gave them a choice to either work in the fields, or to remain within their houses and pray.

The Restoration in England in 1660 relaxed Puritan strictures, but a religious suspicion of sports remained to become a part of Victorian morality in the nineteenth century. John Adams (1735–1826) of Massachusetts, the second president of the United States, claimed, "I was not sent to this world to spend my days in sports, diversions, and pleasures. I was born for business; for both activity and study." Ironically, evangelical Protestant Christianity embraced sports in the latter part of the nineteenth century as a proper expression of God's will and missionaries became a major channel for the spread of modern sports in the world. Still, supported by local "blue laws" the Puritan insistence to keep Sunday free of sports, public entertainments, and business lingered into the latter part of the twentieth century.

At the current time evidence of religion in sport remains. Individual athletes who are dedicated Christians cross themselves or pray on the playing fields. Sports Ambassadors (1952– ), Fellowship of Christian Athletes

(1954– ) and Athletes in Action (1966– ) use athletics to spread Christianity. A small group of athletes have proclaimed a Black Muslim faith and some Jewish athletes—notably Hank Greenberg in 1934 and Sandy Koufax in 1965—refuse to play baseball on the holy day of Yom Kippur. At the invocation before an American football game between the Miami Dolphins and the Atlanta Falcons in the 1970s the Archbishop Coleman F. Carroll implored: "We sometimes get blitzed by heavy sorrows or red-dogged by Satan. Teach us to run the right patterns in our life so that we will truly make a touchdown one day through the heavenly gates as the angels and saints cheer us on from the sidelines." The United States Supreme Court forbade prayers in public schools in 1962, but prayers before games were common in America until gradually foregone in the 1980s and 1990s as improper for a pluralistic society. In 2000 the US Supreme Court prohibited student led prayer before high school football games.

*[handwritten margin note: Praying is common in sporting events]*

*[handwritten margin note: Religion is always present]*

Pageantry with religious fervor, nevertheless, takes place at the Olympic festival—flags, music, fireworks, flights of pigeons, parades, the oath of athletes, and the Olympic torch run introduced in 1934 that ends with the lighting of a symbolic flame. There is pageantry with costumes during the halftimes of athletic contests and at the big championship games at season's end. There are also rituals of school songs, logos to profess loyalty, chants, and special days such as homecoming. There is, moreover, a passionate commitment by followers. Catholic theologian Michael Novak argues that in America sports are a natural religion, a form of godliness—"a faith without an explanation, a love without a rationale"—that people either feel and understand, or they don't. He argues, "Human life is essentially a defeat; we die. The victories of sport are ritual triumphs of grace, agility, perfection, beauty over death." And, "One does not play for the sake of *work*; one plays for the sake of excellence. The point of the excellence is that there is no point. Against the darkness, it is all we have."

Sociologists and journalists have pointed out similar characteristics of religions and sports in the West. Charles S. Prebish, a Buddhist scholar, writing in the *Antioch Review* in 1984 summarized the issue:

> What it boils down to is this: if sport can bring its advocates to an experience of the ultimate, and this (pursuit and) experience is expressed through a formal series of public and private rituals requiring a symbolic language and space deemed sacred by its worshipers, then it is both proper and necessary to call sport itself a religion.

*[handwritten margin note: sport itself is comparable to a religion]*

Religion has been an influence on sporting events from an early period in human existence, both as an inspiration for sporting events, and as an influence upon how the sport was conducted. It is ironic that in the contemporary world, sport itself might be considered a religion, but it is something that many people of traditional faiths would refuse to recognize and even consider sacrilegious.

## Entertainment

The pleasure of participating in a sport, or the enjoyment of witnessing athletic activity is also a phenomenon of traditional sports. There is little known about the interaction between athlete and audience, or about spectators in general before the twentieth century, only glimpses of their presence. Excited Assyrian nobles witnessing the hunting scenes of King Asshurbanipal (669–640 BCE) are depicted in the relief carvings on the temple walls at Nineveh; at Karnak in Egypt a granite inscription announces about Amenophis II, "His majesty performed these feats before the eyes of the whole land," meaning in front of the nobles and the army; at Medinet Habu in Egypt there is a frieze from 1160 BCE that shows a grandstand of animated nobles and foreign dignitaries following the activities of ten pairs of wrestlers featuring Egyptians fighting against prisoners of war; large audiences painted in a fresco at Knossos in Crete (1500 BCE) watch ceremonial performances.

The Greeks, Etruscans, and Romans provided stadiums to stage mass entertainment. In the tradition of the ancient Olympic Games heralds sent from Olympia by the Elian hosts announced the time of the games and a truce of one to three months so that spectators might travel to the site. War, legal disputes, and executions were forbidden to ensure the safe passage of athletes and fans. Since the site lay in the countryside the hosts had to provide food, water, and camping facilities. Epictetus, a first century Stoic philosopher, commented:

> There are enough irksome and troublesome things in life; aren't things just as bad at the Olympic festival? Aren't you scorched there by the fierce heat? Aren't you crushed in the crowd? Isn't it difficult to freshen yourself up? Doesn't the rain soak you to the skin? Aren't you bothered by the noise, the din and other nuisances? But it seems to me that you are well able to bear and indeed gladly endure all this, when you think of the gripping spectacles that you will see.

Lucian (117–180 CE), a Greek satirist and writer, explained the excitement of a fan:

> If the Olympic Games were being held now . . . you would be able to see for yourself why we attach such great importance to athletics. No one can describe in mere words the extraordinary . . . pleasure derived from them and which you yourself would enjoy if you were

seated among the spectators feasting your eyes on the prowess and stamina of the athletes, the beauty and power of their bodies, their incredible dexterity and skill, their invincible strength, their courage, ambition, endurance and tenacity. You would never stop . . . applauding them.

Roman leaders provided entertaining "circus" celebrations of chariot racing, fights with fierce animals, and bloody gladiator contests for a restless and largely unemployed city population. These celebrations reflected the warlike nature of the Roman Empire and the general violence of existence when the average lifespan reached only 25 years. Chariot teams designated by color—white, red, green, and blue—attracted fan loyalty, organized cheering, and gambling. Historian Ammianus Marcellinus (330–390 CE) wrote:

> Now let me describe for you this mass of people, unemployed and therefore with too much time on their hands. For them the Circus Maximus [the Roman chariot arena] is temple, home, social club and center of all their hopes. You can see them beyond the city, arguing about the races . . . and declaring that the country will come to ruin unless their favorite wins in the next races. And on the day they all rush to the circus even before daybreak, to secure a place.

At times the crowd could help decide the fate of a fallen gladiator—with thumbs up for mercy or thumbs down for death—but the Roman presentations were mainly for mass entertainment and the political popularity of the organizer. The acceptance of women as spectators and participants varied. Women sat mixed with men in Rome. Although there were some female gladiators by and large the participants and the audiences were male. Women were formally excluded either as spectators or participants from the Olympic Games and from the chariot contests in Constantinople. As the tourneys of the latter Middle Ages in Europe became increasingly a mock battle with rules, however, upper-class female spectators became an object of chivalry. The estimated largest attendance at the tournaments was no more than 2,000 people.

Fan violence was not unknown. American Indian lacrosse games offer a mild example. Native women were active spectators who hit their men with tree branches to inspire the players' full effort. After all, the household goods had been gambled upon the outcome. The Byzantine Empire provides a shocking example. Emperor Justinian (482–565) sparked the infamous Nika riot at Constantinople in 532 when he tried to suppress armed chariot fans at the Hippodrome. It boiled over into an aborted attempt to overthrow the emperor, and ultimately resulted in a torched city with 30,000 dissidents slaughtered by Justinian's soldiers in the stadium. Such distant events provide "snapshots" about fan behavior, but much more is known about fan violence from the sociological studies of "hooliganism" in the mid-twentieth century.

## Geography

A few geographers have taken up questions about the locations of various sports and the consequences. For the most part their focus has been upon current sports in the West, but questions about location and space for athletic activities pertain to pre-modern sports as well. Macro-geographic considerations are obvious. Ice and winter sports developed where there was a cold climate that provided an abundance of frozen lakes and snow. Aquatic sports would likely be found on tropical islands or places with accommodating coastlines. Hot, dry desert climates dictated caution about exposure of the human body. Herodotus (485–425 BCE), the wandering Greek historian, noted that people of the Middle East kept their bodies covered and unlike the Greeks thought that nudity was shameful. This was probably a climatic necessity, but it should be noted that the ancient Egyptians seemed to have had no such compulsion in the desert heat of the Nile Valley.

Micro-geographic considerations can be made for specific places. The Mayans and the Minoans, for instance, placed their ball and bull courts near temple sites. The Greeks, moreover, thought that every city worth being considered a "polis" had to have a reserved open space for physical and intellectual exercise. Called a *gymnasion* the space compared to modern city parks with trees, open areas, water supply, and buildings for indoor meetings. Athens possessed three such *gymnasions* and it was at or near these places that the great Greek philosophers—Socrates, Plato, and Aristotle—held their conversations and established their schools. The Greeks believed in a harmony of mind and body and it seemed appropriate that intellectual and physical training should progress together in the same place. The location of at least two of their Panhellenic games, Delphi and Olympia, lay in the countryside at holy places. Delphi was actually mountainous and the place of the Temple of Apollo with its famous oracle that could provide advice and predictions about life was on a slope. Its stadium and hippodrome had to be constructed a short distance away from the temple in order to find a suitable flat area.

The Etruscans built the Circus Maximus, a stadium for chariot races, inside their capital city; it was substantially expanded by the Romans once they conquered the Etruscans. The three-tiered, 200,000-seat Circus Maximus, the largest stadium until modern times, along with the 50,000-seat Colesseum, completed in 82 CE, dominated the central portions of

Rome. They underscored the importance of spectacular sports in Roman life, and indeed, the ruins of the ancient Colesseum symbolize even today the glories of the Roman Empire to modern tourists. Roman governors were expected to build stadiums in the provinces, and in the eastern remnant of the Roman Empire that became the Byzantine Empire at Constantinople the Hippodrome occupied a position near the tip of the peninsula close to a complex of palaces. Designed for chariot racing with space for some 50,000 fans the Hippodrome had a median down the center of the track known as the "spina." It was an assembly point where common folk could see the emperor, where executions took place, where theatrical presentations occurred, and where the popular chariot races were run. The Hippodrome was the locus, the "spine" of the empire, and the pulse point where the Nika riot began.

Until the advent of modern sports, nowhere else in the world could such large stadiums with extensive seating for mass spectators be found—not in Asia, not in Africa, not in North America, not in South America. Traditional sports elsewhere took place at convenient places—a clearing in the forest for American Indians; a market space for sub-Saharan African wrestlers; castle towns for Medieval European tournaments; Shinto temples for Sumo wrestlers.

## Eros   —→ *the erotic aspect of sport is clearly a draw*

The erotic aspect of sports is a taboo subject, yet it exists. Allen Guttmann, one of the foremost writers of sports history, argues that the joy of sports to some degree involves eros, the sexual force that attracts people to one another. He readily admits the difficulty of separating pornography from eroticism, and advises, "Since the search for objective criteria distinguishing the erotic from the pornographic has led to interminable haggles, ill will, legislative stalemate, split hairs, and a divided judiciary, the best way out of the definitional *cul de sac* seems to be a frank acceptance of subjectivity. . . . " It is, thus, an issue for individuals to decide for themselves.

In art, both the ancient Egyptians and Greeks rejected overweight people, and the Greeks adopted an athlete as the ideal male for their statues. The Athenians had no hesitancy concerning nudity and decorated their trade pottery with active naked athletes. The participants of the Olympic Games performed nude. According to legend, in 720 BCE a sprinter named Orsippos lost his loincloth in a race and discovered that a naked man could run faster than others. After this, led by the Spartans, everyone took off their clothes. Women were not allowed to view the games, but this seems to be more an attitude about the retiring role of women in society than one of prudery. According to Plutarch, Lykourgos, a legendary lawgiver of Sparta, was an exception:

Lykourgos exercised the bodies of the virgins with footraces and wrestling and throwing the discus and the javelin so that their offspring might grow forth from strong roots in strong bodies, and so that they might be patient and strong in childbirth and struggle well and easily with the pains. He removed from them all softness and daintiness and effeminacy and accustomed the girls no less than the boys to parade in the nude and to dance and sing at certain religious festivals in the presence of the young men as spectators. . . .

Plutarch also mentioned that such customs were a stimulus for marriage. Probably so considering the circumstances, but beyond the Greeks there is not much recorded about the connection of eros and sports in historical documents. Plato wrote in *The Symposium* about a failed homoerotic attempt to seduce Socrates in a wrestling match; successful Roman gladiators were known to attract highborn women, such as the one that archaeologists discovered in the ashes of Pompeii in the gladiator barracks; males in Nubia wrestled to prove dominance and attract females; Tamil tribesmen of southern India tried to prove virility by throwing a bull to the ground while women lined the corral fence to choose their husbands from the survivors; in the smock races of eighteenth-century Europe lower class women stripped to underclothes and ran for the reward of a dress and possibly a husband.

Eroticism in sports is much more apparent in contemporary times such as in the phenomenon of body building competition, or in the famous sports film about the 1936 Olympics by Leni Riefenstahl. "To admire the aesthetic dimension of the sequence [on diving] and of the film as if it were unrelated to eros is foolish reductionism," says Guttmann. "There is no more erotic sports film than *Olympia*, a cinematic declaration of love if there ever was one." Guttmann's major point that eros in sports has been ignored is well taken. Eros is not the only influence on traditional sports as Guttmann would agree, but it is something that should not be denied.

## Conclusion

Without the inherent athletic imperative sports likely would not exist. Of all the secondary influences on the shape and style of traditional sports— vocation, war, religion, entertainment, geography, and eros—probably warfare is the most important. The other elements are present, however, with varying amounts of influence. In the modern period a powerful third level of influences has directed the evolution of sports.

Inherent athletic imperative

Secondary

## Further reading

Roger Bannister, *First Four Minutes* (London: Sportsmans Book Club, 1956); Eliot J. Gorn, "The Social Significance of Gouging in the Southern Backcountry," in Steven A. Riess (ed.), *Major Problems in American Sport History* (Boston: Houghton Mifflin, 1997), pp. 62–70; Allen Guttmann, *The Erotic in Sports* (New York: Columbia, 1996); Allen Guttmann and Lee Thompson, *Japanese Sports, a History* (Honolulu: Hawaii, 2001); Bernd Heinrich, *Racing the Antelope* (New York: Harper Collins, 2001); Homer, *The Iliad*, trans. E. V. Rieu (Middlesex: Penguin, 1950); John Jerome, *The Sweet Spot in Time* (New York: Touchstone, 1980); Benjamin Lowe, *The Beauty of Sport* (Englewood Cliffs, New Jersey: Prentice Hall, 1977); Michael Novak, *The Joy of Sports* (New York: Basic Books, 1976); Vera Olivova, *Sports and Games in the Ancient World* (New York: St Martin's, 1984); Charles Prebish, "Heavenly Fathers, Divine Goalie: Sports and Religion," *Antioch Review*, 42 (1984) pp. 316–318. Karl B. Raitz (ed.), *The Theater of Sport* (Baltimore: Johns Hopkins, 1995); George Sheehan, *Running and Being* (New York: Simon and Schuster, 1978); George Sheehan, *Personal Best* (Emmaus: Pennsylvania: Rochdale Press, 1989); Judith Swaddling, *The Ancient Olympic Games* (Austin: Texas, 1980).

Two influences on creation of sport

● Most significantly, humans are born w/ the necessity to develop inherent athleticism

● Secondary aspects: vocation
religion
eros
geography
WAR - most significant

# Chapter 3

# The Emergence of Modern Sports

*[handwritten: Modern Sports produced by modern age of industry]*

Modern sports appeared during the great societal shifts that accompanied the industrial revolution in Great Britain and the United States. As twentieth century scholars studied sports they noted this emergence, analyzed it, attempted to select the most important activities, and pursued the history of individual sports. This chapter essentially tracks that endeavor.

## Pre-modern and modern sports

There is a notable difference between the traditional, or pre-modern sports, and the modern sports of the nineteenth and twentieth centuries. Compare, for instance, the lacrosse game of the American Indians with the modern game played by collegians today. Hundreds of Indians took to the field to scramble for the ball with a stick in each hand. Today, rules limit the teams to ten-a-side for men and twelve-a-side for women using one stick each. The Indians played in a convenient, natural clearing with goals 250 yards distant—some accounts say miles apart—and now the field is limited to 100 yards. The Indians related the game directly to religion and warfare; today such connections are obscure, if not divorced from the playing. For the Indians it was mainly a male endeavor, but now either sex plays the game. To be sure, there is a distant similarity between traditional and modern lacrosse, but there are major differences in rules, venues, equipment, motives, gender, scheduling, records, and the social strata of the players. *[handwritten margin note: Modern Sports extremely organized in comparison to traditional sports]*

English sociologists Norbert Elias and Eric Dunning along with American historian Allen Guttmann have noted these comparative differences between old and new sports in their writings. Elias, a German-Jew whose mother died at the Nazi death camp of Auschwitz in World War II, was understandably engrossed about the nature of violence. He inquired:

> What kind of societies are they, one may ask, where people in great numbers and almost worldwide enjoy, as actors or spectators, physical contests between individual people or teams of people and the tensions,

the excitement engendered by these contests where no blood flows and no serious harm is done to each other by the contestants?

He developed a theory about a "civilizing process" in which people gradually learned to contain emotion and aggression. He offered as an example the use of gloves, weight divisions, and other such rules in boxing to protect the athletes and reduce bloodshed. Eric Dunning, his student and colleague, carried Elias' work into the study of contemporary fan violence.

Allen Guttmann in *From Ritual to Record* (1978) provided further analysis about the attributes of modern sports. These characteristics included: secularism (non-religious); equality (equal rules for all participants); bureaucratization (organizational control); specialization (specific positions and roles played in the game); rationalization (rules and training for efficient skills); quantification (an emphasis upon measurement by numbers); and record keeping (with the thought of continual improvement). Historians Melvin L. Adelman and Steven A. Riess added the use of publicity and public announcements to the list. The ideas of these scholars are widely accepted by sports historians at the present time and they are an endorsement of the use of modernization theory as a structure for analysis.

Behind these attributes, however, were forces of societal change that made possible, if not impelled, the transformation from traditional to modern sport. Hand in hand with the industrial revolution (1775 onwards) came a surge in world population. Mass production needed the mass markets that could be found in a global economy. The industrial revolution not only brought about the growth of factory towns, but also brought technical changes in agriculture that provided more food with less labor. This allowed and encouraged a massive demographic shift of people from the countryside to the town.

When it started, only about 3 percent of the world population lived in urban places. In 1900, Great Britain, the initial leader of the industrial revolution, became the first nation with half its population living in cities. The United States reached that point in 1920, and the world is turning one-half urban at the present moment. The phenomenon of industrial growth meant that people, especially the middle and upper classes, gradually became possessed of more money and leisure time. The phenomenon of urban growth meant that there was a compact population that welcomed, if not needed, diversion and entertainment. This provided a clear stage for the growth of sports.

Technology and rationalization—knowledge applied to industrial production—affected sports as well. The vulcanization of rubber in 1839, for example, led to solid rubber bicycle wheels and eventually to the balloon tires used today. Rationalization of the bicycle during the latter part of the nineteenth century brought about spoked wheels, diamond-shaped frames, chain drives, and gearing while mass production drove the price down within reach of the middle class. For the amount of energy expended by the rider, the bicycle became the most efficient form of transportation ever invented. In 1900, moreover, bicycle racers were the most exciting and highest paid professional athletes in the United States and Europe. Symbolically, the foremost bicycle race in the world, the Tour de France that covered 2,500–3,000 miles in two weeks, began in 1903.

For sports rationalization also brought about organizations to regulate the activity with rules and to promote it with contests. The governing associations not only promulgated regulations, they kept records and publicized their actions. The organizations, in other words, became bureaucratic agencies with their own internal politics and external ambitions. Important marking points in the development of any modern sport, therefore, are the dates and place of the first organizing group dedicated to the sport. Quite frequently these bureaucracies demonstrated tenacious longevity and control. In addition, the development of a sport often started with the upper classes and filtered downward to the lower classes. It was the upper class that had the time and money; the lower class had neither.

## Modern sports and the West

Historical researchers indicate that modern sport began in the West, especially in Great Britain and the United States. It is thus understandable that the characteristics of modern sports outlined by Allen Guttmann for the most part are those of capitalism and the industrial revolution. Many of the sports, not all but many, involved in international competition today are sports that originated, organized, and diffused from the West. This opens the door to charges that the history of modern sports is Eurocentric. Well, yes that is true, but the facts that soccer began in the boy's schools of Great Britain, and basketball began at a YMCA training school in the United States cannot be changed. These are the two most widespread sports in the world today and they are from the West.

Other people and nations have adopted, and adapted these activities. There are crude soccer fields to be seen in jungle clearings of villages in the Amazon and basketball backstops with hoops for pickup games on the docks of Chinese ports. As soccer has become a "people's game" no longer dominated by Great Britain, so also basketball is becoming a "people's game" slipping away from the predominance of the United States. In this sense, modern sport is no longer Eurocentric; it is global.

Modern sport has become global

## Sports in the modern world

There is no definitive way to enumerate the most important global sports. Maarten Van Bottenburg, the director of a Dutch social research company, attempted this task for his book *Global Games* (2001), found himself hindered by insufficient data, and turned to the quantity of specific sports organizations. The simple number of national associations for a sport indicated that the top ten sports were volleyball, track and field, soccer, basketball, tennis, boxing, table tennis, judo, swimming, and cycling. He distrusted the broad informal surveys that indicated walking and swimming as the most popular participant sports as too vague and unreliable. Others may not agree.

In regard to spectators, contemporary sources indicate that in the United States the most popular sports are American football, baseball, basketball, boxing, car racing, tennis, track and field, and golf. Soccer and cricket reign in England. In Europe the top sports shows are soccer, the Olympics, tennis, formula 1 car racing, and basketball. Soccer and swimming are most important in Asia; soccer is significant for South America; rugby, cricket, and Australian football lead in Australia. Roughly then, the important modern global sports at present are soccer, basketball, tennis, track and field, volleyball and to a lesser extent American football, cricket, baseball, rugby, skiing, boxing, judo, car racing, cycling, swimming, and table tennis.

## Horse racing

The first modern sport to develop, however, was horse racing. Seemingly, wherever people possessed horses, there was horse racing and it most certainly had roots in traditional sports. Consider this episode from the frontier history of the American West. At Fort Chadbourne north of San Angelo, Texas, some army officers challenged a band of Comanche Indians to a horse race. The Indians appeared reluctant to compete against a Thoroughbred Kentucky mare, but placed some bets and brought out a longhaired, miserable looking "sheep of a pony." The Indian horse was a mustang, a mixture of Spanish, African, and Arabian breeds that had roamed wild over the plains for a century and a half. Although small, the breed was known for its toughness and endurance.

When a 170-pound Indian jockey carrying a club mounted the small Mustang, the soldiers good-naturedly substituted their third best horse. The mustang won and the Comanches took the flour, sugar, and coffee that had been bet against their buffalo robes. The officers demanded a second race, put in their second-best horse, and again the Mustang with its heavy rider won. The outraged soldiers then brought out the Kentucky mare and the betting became heavy. This time the Indian jockey gave a yell, threw down the club, bolted into the lead, and fifty yards from the finish line turned around on his horse and made obscene gestures at the American loser. As writer Mark Twain once noted, "It is difference of opinion that makes horse races," and horse racing held worldwide fascination.

Gambling, which can sharpen the interest in a sporting event, has been linked with horse racing from the beginning and is one of the major reasons for its development into a modern sport. There had to be assurance that a race was fair or gamblers would not risk their money. Therefore, betting people began to demand standard rules for racing and in 1750 wealthy aristocrats in Great Britain formed the Jockey Club of London to set rules, appoint officials, and conduct fair races. Already, horse racing was widespread in Great Britain—there were over 100 towns holding regular races by 1722. Tattersalls, a market for buying and selling racehorses opened in London in 1766 and in 1770 James Weatherby began publishing the *Racing Calendar* which popularized rules of racing and printed a schedule of events. "Classic" races of one mile to a mile and a half evolved for 3-year-old Thoroughbreds—St Leger in 1778, the Oaks in 1779, the Derby in 1780, the 2000 Guineas in 1809, and the 1000 Guineas in 1814. For all the watchfulness, however, chicanery still took place. One of the more notorious scandals was that of Running Rein.

In 1844 at the Epsom Derby in England, a race designated for 3-year-old horses, a horse called Running Rein won. A problem arose afterwards because it became known that Running Rein was really a 4-year-old horse named Maccabaeus. During the race Running Rein kicked another illegal 4-year-old called Leander so badly that it had to be destroyed. The owners of Leander cut off its lower jaw afterwards in a botched attempt to hide its age. Investigators alleged, moreover, that William Crockford, a gaming house owner had taken large bets from a syndicate that was in on the substitutions. Crockford had died the morning of the race, however, and all bets should have been called off. The conspirators, nonetheless, dressed the corpse and propped the body in a chair so that passersby would think it only an old man asleep in a chair. They later reported that Crockford had died that night after the race. Exposure of the scandal led to a consensus that British racing had to be more closely supervised. The Jockey Club of London led the reform, gained acceptance of its code of conduct, and by 1850 emerged as the virtual arbiter of British horse racing. There have been other scandals over time, nevertheless, and all horse racing still carries with it a faint odor of corruption.

In colonial America plantation owners bet heavily on quarter horse races —an all-out sprint between horses on a quarter-mile dirt track. The track was often a street or a country road; it was too expensive at first to clear trees to build a large racecourse. In Virginia, where horses were considered an expression of the character of the owner, the owners often challenged each other in match races. Colonialists imported some 150 Thoroughbred stallions by the time of the American Revolution and horse racing became the first national sports spectacle in the young United States.

Quarter-mile races gave way to longer endurance races on mile-long dirt tracks in the early nineteenth century. In 1823 a match race that reflected the widening political split between the northern and southern sections of the country took place on Long Island near New York City. Some 60,000 fans showed up to watch the northern horse American Eclipse beat Sir Henry in two of three four-mile heats. Young bon vivant John Cox Stevens from New York bet his purse, watch, and diamond breastpin on the race, won, and afterwards purchased both horses for his private stable at Hoboken.

Interrupted by the American Civil War when both horses and men went to war, Thoroughbred racing rebounded with the establishment of special races for 3-year-olds—the Belmont in Westchester County, New York in 1867, the Preakness in Baltimore in 1873, and the Kentucky Derby at Louisville in 1875. These became the Triple Crown of horseracing in the United States. The greatest Triple Crown winner was Secretariat (1970–1989) who came from last place to win the Kentucky Derby in 1973 in record time. At the Preakness he came from six horse lengths behind to win by two lengths. At the Belmont the jockey just let him run and Secretariat won by an astonishing 31 lengths with a world record in the mile and a half race of 2 minutes 24 seconds.

Over time a variety of equestrian sports emerged—steeplechase, dressage, gymkhana, Thoroughbred, harness, fox hunting, rodeo, endurance, polo—all with rules, regulations, and controlling organizations. Horse lineage, particularly of Thoroughbreds, became important with breeders and clubs maintaining meticulous records. All Thoroughbreds, worldwide, for example, are known to descend from three stallions imported to Great Britain from the Near East—Byerley Turk (1680), Darley Arabian (1700) and Godolphin Barb (1724). The owners bred them with local English stock. British jockeys in the late nineteenth century adopted the American style of riding called "monkey-on-a-stick" where the saddle was pushed forward, reins and stirrups shortened, and the jockey rode with bent knees. The American Jockey Club, however, did not form until 1894, and in the United States racing was controlled by state racing commissions. With all of the historical complications, therefore, horse racing became the first modern sport.

## Cricket

While horse racing developed, so also did cricket, the first of the major bat and ball games. The origin as well as the name is obscure, but it may have evolved from the peasant game of stool ball where a milkmaid defended a milking stool with a broom while another tried to knock it over with an improvised ball. The earliest reference to cricket dates from 1598 and it became popular in southeastern England in the seventeenth century. It was the first team sport in which upper-class sportsmen exerted themselves without the use of a horse. Besides, the bowling (throwing the ball at the stumps to knock off the bails balanced on top) could be assigned to a hired hand of the estate.

The aristocrats who placed bets of up to 10,000 pounds on games began to draft pre-game regulations and by the end of the century there were standards for bats, balls, stumps, bails, the size of the wicket, and for playing the game. Women participated in the eighteenth century, but by the end of the nineteenth century cricket was considered a man's game to the exclusion of women. As it increased in popularity a London club of the 1730s evolved into the Marylebone Cricket Club (MCC) that was established in 1787. Although it changed places several times the home cricket ground of the MCC, known as Lord's, became the mecca of world cricket, and the MCC itself became the world's governing authority.

The rules of 1835 required an underhanded pitch, but the quicker overhanded throw became popular and was allowed by the MCC in 1864. The bowler who delivered with a smooth, straight-arm motion after a short run usually bounced the ball off the turf. This required a carefully tended, smooth grassy playing surface, and Lord's hired its first groundskeeper the same year. Cricket, as it developed, was played on a large oval field with the center of action on a ten-foot-wide, twenty-two-yards-long rectangular pitch area in the center. At each end of the pitch was a "crease" in which stood a wicket made up of three closely spaced pointed stumps pushed into the ground with two bails, or wooden blocks, balanced between the tops. The bowler hurled a glancing, hard leather-covered ball off the ground and tried to knock off the bails. If the batsman did not protect the wicket and the bails were dislodged, the batter was out. The batsman was also out if his fly ball was caught before it touched the ground, an opponent knocked off the bails with a ball in hand while the batsman was outside the crease, the batter blocked the pathway to the wicket with his body (leg before wicket), he hit the ball twice or with his hand, or the batter inadvertently broke the wicket by touching it.

The batsman could score runs by hitting the ball in any direction and running safely to the opposite crease. If a ball was hit outside the field of play it was worth six runs, if it went outside on the bounce it was worth four runs. Two batsmen were on the field at once and they had to cross safely to the opposite crease for an in-field run to count, but the batsmen did not have to run even if the ball was hit. Teams consisted of eleven players and when ten were out the inning was over and the fielding team had its turn at bat. As one wit put it: "When they are all out the side that is out comes in and the side that's been in goes out and tries to get those coming in out. . . . When both sides have been in and out . . . that is the end of the game." Test matches (championships) consisted of two innings, could last five days with eight to ten hours of play per day, and might record over 500 runs scored per team. It was considered remarkable, but not impossible, for a player to score a "century," or 100 runs.

William Gilbert Grace (1848–1915), England's greatest cricketer of the nineteenth century scored 126 centuries and almost 55,000 runs in his 40-year career. He grew up near Bristol, the son of a successful country doctor who loved the game. The press first noticed Grace in 1864 at age 15 when he scored 170 and 56 in a match at Hove. On his way to breaking every cricket record he shocked contemporaries with his shaggy beard, growing waistline, and unclean body. Viscount Cobham, another player, said that Grace had the dirtiest neck he had ever seen. Grace, moreover, strode around the field bellowing at umpires and distracting opponents with a high-pitched giggle. Although officially an amateur he wagered on matches, accepted testimonials, and organized paying tours. Yet, he worked hard at his sport and played with a fierce enthusiasm. In 1895 he began the season by staying at bat for an entire day. Small boys followed him about, adults cheered his prowess, and he became England's first national sports hero.

Cricket, like American baseball, is said to be a simple game—the team that scores the most runs wins the game. But, to a newcomer the rules are bewildering and the long matches unconscionable. Lord Mancroft, a British politician, wrote in 1979: "Cricket—a game which the English, not being a spiritual people, have invented in order to give themselves some conception of eternity." Cricket, nevertheless, became the national pastime of England and spread throughout the British Empire. Historian John Arlott noticed that, as long as 200 years ago, landscape painters who had little knowledge of the game included a cricket match as a part of the scene. It is a mystery, however, why cricket failed to take root in the United States and Canada.

## Baseball

Although there were cricket clubs in the United States in the nineteenth century the bat and ball game of baseball supplanted them. American baseball originated in rules supplied by stool ball, rounders, and town ball—folk games that had roots in England. These games used some sort of a stick to defend a stool or base, and stakes or poles to run around after the batter struck the ball. Alexander J. Cartrwright (1820–1892), who was a 25-year-old bank clerk in New York City, organized the Knickerbocker Base Ball Club in 1845, drew up a set of rules inspired by the various street games, and played the first game of baseball at James Cox Steven's recreational area at Hoboken. It was a social event for middle-class gentlemen who wore blue wool pants, white flannel shirts, and straw hats. They held a dinner after the game and spectators came by invitation only.

Compared to cricket baseball was quicker, there was more action, and for the United States baseball patriotically suited a strengthening nation that took pride in its own inventions. Other teams formed as the popularity of the "New York Game" spread and 22 teams in 1857 founded the National Association of Base Ball Players (NABBP) to take charge of rule changes. It was a myth perpetrated by baseball enthusiast and equipment manufacturer Albert G. Spalding that Abner Doubleday invented baseball in Cooperstown, New York in 1839.

The Civil War helped to spread the game throughout the nation as bored Union soldiers sought entertainment and taught local boys to play the game. The Cincinnati Red Stockings, the first professional team, took to the new transcontinental railroad in 1869 to introduce baseball to California. There, spectators fired their pistols in the air to see if they could get an intimidated fielder to miss a ball. To control the schedules, rules, and the business of baseball two major professional leagues formed. William A. Hulbert of Chicago put together the National League in 1876 and Byron Bancroft Johnson formed the American League in 1899. They competed for spectators for several years and then signed a truce in 1903. They agreed on rules, exclusive contract rights to players, franchises for cities, and a World Series championship.

By this time the rules were mainly agreed upon: a diamond shaped infield with bases 90 feet apart; a pitcher in the center of the diamond who threw a ball to the batter at home plate who could receive four balls or three strikes; outs came with three strikes, thrown out at a base, tagged between bases, a caught fly ball; runs counted when a player crossed home base; nine persons per team; three outs per inning; nine innings per game. The players used a rounded bat and mitts unlike cricket players who used a flat edged bat and no gloves. Cricket players thought the use of gloves was "unmanly," and the flat edged bat gave greater control for the placement of the ball while hitting.

The building of playing fields came during waves of enthusiasm for the game. Team owners built early professional baseball stadiums out of wood on cheap land at the end of trolley car lines. They provided some seats under a cover for shade, but most were exposed to the weathering effects of rain and sunshine—hence, the name "bleachers" for cheap stadium seats. Average attendance was 4,000 spectators, mainly middle-class, who paid 50 cents per ticket. In 1908 Jack Norworth, a vaudevillian, wrote "Take Me Out to the Ballgame," a song that became the ritual hymn of baseball sung everywhere after six and a half innings (seventh-inning stretch) when the fans stood to limber up their legs. As the teams prospered, particularly in the big cities, the owners constructed better stadiums of concrete and iron or steel in Detroit (1912), Boston (1912), Chicago (1914), and New York (1923). A second major wave of building began in the 1960s and a third wave came in the 1990s.

The history of American baseball is replete with records and statistics, and the stories of goats, comics, and heroes. There is no other sport that has inspired so much literature as baseball with perhaps the exception of cricket. After hitting a homerun a player is required to round the bases. Herman "Germany" Schaefer who played for the Detroit Tigers in the early twentieth century, however, hit a home run and then instead of simply trotting around the bases he took the opportunity to slide into every base as if it were a close play.

In 1919 Casey Stengel (1889–1975) before he became a storied and long-lived manager played centerfielder for the Pittsburgh Pirates. He had been traded to the Pirates by the Brooklyn Dodgers and in a return game the jeering was rough. Stengel, however, had been given a small bird by a former Brooklyn teammate and he put the bird under his cap. When he came to bat he tipped his hat to the unruly crowd and the bird flew out to the delight of the fans. Yogi Berra, catcher for the New York Yankees from the late 1940s into the 1960s, became noted for his quips, "It's déjà vu all over again," "You can observe a lot by watching," "Baseball is 90 percent mental, the other half is physical," and "It ain't over 'til it's over." Babe Ruth and Jackie Robinson, however, became the greatest heroes of the game.

George Herman "Babe" Ruth (1895–1948) grew up as an incorrigible youth in Baltimore and learned to play baseball at the St Mary's Industrial Home for Boys. In 1914 he began his career as a left-handed pitcher for the Baltimore Orioles. He shortly switched to the Boston Red Sox, gave up pitching for hitting, and started playing for the New York Yankees in 1920. He swung a heavy 44-ounce bat, reached for home runs, and often succeeded. Attendance at Yankee games jumped from 600,000 per year to 1,000,000, and when Yankee Stadium opened in 1923, it was nicknamed "the House the Ruth Built." In 1927 he set a home run record of 60, a record not broken until 1961.

Ruth became an American sports hero and legend. He came from a humble background, possessed an outgoing personality, and truly loved the numberless kids who swarmed over him wherever he went. He lived an uninhibited life, called everyone "Kid," because he couldn't remember names, and depended on raw physical talent. "I get back to the dugout and they ask me what it was I hit and I tell 'em, I don't know except it looked good." He introduced the country to dramatic home run, "big bang" baseball which was aided by the introduction of the "jack rabbit" ball.

Over the preceding decade technology improved the ball with a cork center, tighter windings, and a tightly bound cowhide cover. The ball could be hit harder and farther than the "dead ball" of earlier times that required placement on the field. Ruth, moreover, was a welcome relief from the "Black Sox" scandal of 1920–1922 that tarnished the nation's beloved game with allegations about eight Chicago White Sox players who fixed the outcome of the 1919 World Series. The new baseball commissioner, Kenesaw Mountain Landis, expelled the players for life even though they had been acquitted by a Chicago jury. Ruth went on to baseball immortality.

Jack Roosevelt "Jackie" Robinson (1919–1971) also a superior ball player gained immortality for a different reason. In spite of a bloody civil war that gave freedom to slaves in America the country remained a segregated society through the first half of the twentieth century. African-Americans by and large lived in separate communities, ate at black-owned restaurants, attended segregated schools, and played on all-black athletic teams. Jim Crow (discrimination) laws and local legislation supported the division of the races. Blacks associated with the dominant white community mainly in the area of business and sometimes in politics. Following World War II when blacks fought for the security of the world and against the prejudice of Adolf Hitler it became obviously illogical to support such narrow mindedness at home.

Branch Rickey (1881–1965) who had become the general manager and part owner of the Brooklyn Dodgers in 1943 thought that black athletes could help his team and he was willing to break the color line. Although there had been outstanding, isolated black athletes—Marshall "Major" Taylor in bicycle racing, Jack Johnson in boxing, Joe Louis in boxing, and Jesse Owens in track—they were exceptions and not enfolded into white society. Years earlier, in 1903, when he was a student-coach of baseball at Ohio Wesleyan, Rickey's first baseman, Charles Thomas, was an African-American. While traveling to South Bend to play Notre Dame, a local hotel refused to provide room for Thomas because of his color. Thomas offered to leave the team and go home, but Rickey refused and obtained a cot for Thomas to stay in the coach's room. While discussing strategy with his captain the night before the game Rickey observed Thomas out of the corner of his eye sitting on the end of the cot, tears running down his face, and compulsively rubbing his hands. "Black skin," muttered Thomas, "black skin. If I could only make 'em white."

Rickey never forgot and was willing to risk changes if he could find the right athlete. "The Negroes will make us winners for years to come," he said, "and for that I will happily bear being called a bleeding heart and a do-gooder and all that humanitarian rot." His scouts found Jackie Robinson, an outstanding University of California at Los Angeles graduate, veteran, and shortstop for the Kansas City Monarchs. The Kansas City team was the best in the black baseball league. Giving him due warning about the social brutalities to come and extracting a promise from the player to hold his

*Robinson's contract required him to hold his temper*

*Broke color line in sports period*

temper, Rickey hired Robinson, sent him for a season to a farm club in Montreal, and then brought him to the Dodger team in 1947.

Rickey and Robinson broke the color barrier in America's most important sport. The fiery Robinson held his temper for two years as he had promised, turned the other cheek, and let his superior skills at base running and batting answer the bigots and critics. He led the Dodgers to a pennant victory and won the first Rookie of the Year award. Other teams woke up and began to recruit talented African-Americans. Black fans poured into the stands and the cracked walls of segregation in American sports and society began to crumble. In this case a dramatic act in the arena of sport reflected what America was and what it could become. The timing was perfect and thus the courage of Jackie Robinson and Branch Rickey had profound social and political consequences.

## Golf and tennis

The development of two other small ball sports, golf and tennis, deserve mention for their later global reach. In their modern context they hold upper-class status as country-club sports with only limited popularity as a "people's game." Nonetheless, golf developed in Scotland, as far as can be determined, from the traditional game of shinty, a Celtic form of field hockey. Upper-class Scots used thorn-tree clubs to hit small leather balls stuffed with boiled feathers down a long grassy fairway into a small hole located on a closely cropped green area. The object was to take the least number of strokes. The word "golf" comes from the Scots word "colf," meaning stick or club, which gives authority to its origin.

*Golf (Scotland) in 17th Century reaches global appeal in modern era*

Scotsmen were playing the game as early as 1457 when James II prohibited it for interfering with archery practice. When James IV of Scotland became James I of England in 1603, however, he built a course at Blackheath to introduce English nobles to the quaint Scottish game. In 1754 the Royal and Ancient Golf Club at St Andrews formed to set the rules for the game and began to carry out the same sort of governing function as the Marylebone Cricket Club did for cricket. In 1764, for example, the Royal and Ancient Golf Club set 18 as the official number of holes for a game.

As was the case for early Scottish courses St Andrews developed on linksland along the coast where the wind had shaped marine sands into an undulating surface of dunes, depressions, and grass patches. Grazing animals kept the grass closely cut and although there were shrubs there were but few trees. These open "links" became an embedded part of the world-wide architecture of golf and so the contemporary fairways, greens, rough sand bunkers, and undulating mounds pay constant tribute to a Scottish heritage.

St Andrews, in addition, opened a ladies' section in 1867 which began a pattern of internal segregation by gender that still lingers today at private clubs. Women had to remain in their place and rarely gained any sort of control or voting right in the club even though on weekdays they often outnumbered the men on the premises. But golf with its pleasant surroundings and moderate physical demands quietly spread and attracted middle-aged and middle to upper-class players. By 1910 there were about a thousand courses scattered about Britain, and a community golf club became an embellishment, if not a social refuge, for people living in expensive commuter suburbs.

Hand in hand with the golf course at the country club was the tennis court. According to the French, *tenez* the French word for "attention" or "take heed" is the origin of the word "tennis," and the French word *l'oeuf* meaning "egg" or "zero" is the origin of the word "love" meaning zero in the unexplainable scoring system used in the game. The words are connected in part to the paddle ball game played by French monks. After a period of popularity in England and France as a game played in an enclosed court during the late medieval and early modern periods of time, the sport languished. It has survived, however, as "real tennis" with a handful of active clubs in the United Kingdom, United States, Australia, and France. The French words also relate to lawn tennis which is the outdoor game most people play today.

Major Walter C. Wingfield began the modern sport in 1874 when he patented in England a game of tennis. For $26 he sold a package that included poles, pegs, balls, racquets, a net, and a set of rules. He prescribed an hour-glass shaped court that was narrow at the five-foot net. The game was a success with wealthy young people who set up the tennis court on the well-manicured grass croquet grounds at country estates. Croquet lawns had no footpaths, bushes, gravel, or undulations and were thus ideal to give tennis balls a "true bounce." Croquet evolved from a French peasant game, jumped to Ireland, and then became popular in England in the middle of the nineteenth century. Tennis, an intruder, took over all the grassy croquet areas. In 1877 the All England Croquet Club, located in the London suburb of Wimbledon, decided to hold a tennis tournament and appointed a committee to revise the rules.

The committee arranged for a rectangular court, 78 by 27 feet; and required players to serve alternative games, win games by at least two points, win six games for a set while leading by two games, and win by the best of three sets. The first Wimbledon tournament attracted only 22 players, but the club decided that it should be an annual event. The committee continued to make rules adjustments and shortly, in 1884, it began sharing responsibilities with the Lawn Tennis Association. For a few years the referee adjusted the height of the net and the service line, but in 1882 the distances were made standard with the net placed at three feet, three inches at the center. In 1884 the committee added women's singles and men's doubles; in 1890 they had players exchange ends after each odd game of each set; in 1913 they added women's doubles and mixed doubles. The game, particularly with modifications to the playing surface, quickly spread across Britain and overseas.

The All England Croquet Club added "and Lawn Tennis Club" to its title and the Lawn Tennis Association added member clubs at a rapid rate— 300 clubs in 1900; 1,000 in 1914; and 3,000 in the late 1930s. Although women were allowed to play the game, it was considered unseemly for them to become too involved. They dressed in fashion with ankle length dresses, hats and hairpieces. Once when an Irish lady lost her hairpiece during a windy rally at Wimbledon, she finished the point, picked up the fake hair "as one would a mouse by the tail" deposited it with the referee, and remarked, "Sure, and it's a wonder it doesn't blow yer real hair off." High-spirited women and competition, however, gradually brought relaxation to the constrictive garment code of women's tennis.

## Table tennis

Table tennis, a spin-off of tennis also developed in England. Indoor miniature "tennis" was played in the 1880s and 1890s as after-dinner entertainment by formally dressed aristocrats who set up a playing table in the dining room or parlor. Nets were made of towels, strings between bottles, or rows of books. Cigar boxes sufficed as paddles and carved champagne corks served as balls. Equipment advances shortly produced a net anchored on either side of a table, a short-handled wooden paddle covered with cork or sandpaper, and a celluloid ball.

The game escaped the drawing rooms of the elite as a table tennis craze swept both England and the United States in the early twentieth century. It was inexpensive and wholesome family fun. Arnold Parker, a star English player, developed some of the early rules and pioneered the double-bounce serve whereby the service ball bounced on both sides of the net. It did not work well, he discovered, to smash the ball directly into your opponent's court with an overhand serve as was done in lawn tennis.

Although the game faded in popularity, in 1922 Ivor Montagu (1904–1984), a Cambridge University student, began to codify the rules, including the double-bounce serve. It took 3 sets of 21 points to win a match with the players alternating 5 serves each. A point was scored when a player hit the ball before the first bounce or after the second bounce, or could not return the ball to the opponent's side. In 1926 Montagu met with representatives from Austria, Germany, Hungary, and Sweden in Berlin and formed the International Table Tennis Federation (ITTF) which held the first world championship in London the same year. Lady Swathling, Montagu's mother, donated a cup for the men's team championship. Players competed in men's and women's singles, men's doubles, and mixed doubles. Women's doubles came in 1928 and the Parker Brothers game company of the United States took out a patent for "Ping-Pong," an onomatopoeic trade label that gave the sport a nickname.

Hungarians dominated the world championships in the early years, particularly Victor Barna who became the most famous star of the sport in the 1930s. He warned of the devastating consequences of a fingerspin serve and brought about the rule that in the initial motion of the serve the ball should rest on the flat palm of the hand. It was then thrown up to be struck with the paddle with no snap of the fingers. Another problem of that time was a strategy of passively hitting the ball back and forth waiting for someone to make a mistake. The result in a 1936 championship was a single point that lasted over two hours. The ITTF had to initiate an "expedite rule" to speed up play.

A technical crisis arose in 1952 when unknown Hiroji Satoh of Japan won using a paddle with a three-quarter inch thick foam rubber surface that returned balls with catapult velocity, and interestingly, made little sound when it struck a ball—no more "ping" and "pong". The ITTF accepted the new sponge, and paddle technology accelerated to the point where fast, aggressive attack play left almost no room for a defensive player.

Table tennis, although it did not attract heavy fan support in the West— most of the spectators at tournaments are other tournament players —nonetheless, became a global people's game with little class, gender, or ethnic discrimination. Even today elite players along with basement fanatics still chase their own errant balls. It was a game played both for recreation and in competition, and perhaps along with basketball can be considered the second most popular game behind soccer. Table tennis became one of China's major sports, popular enough to be called a national pastime, and the source of its first world championship. Rong Guotuan won at singles in 1959 in Dortmund, Germany and according to Chinese physical educators "smashed the myth that world championships were unattainable by the Chinese."

## Large ball games

Sports involving small balls were important, but sports involving large balls, the size of basketballs, also became significant to the world. The Indians of Mesoamerica played their mysterious court game with a large ball, as did the Chinese who played *cuju*, a kind of soccer, for military training during the Tang Dynasty (618–907). Renaissance Italian gentlemen played *calico*, a large ball game, on cobblestone piazzas and considered it more serious than war. When the Prince of Orange and his army fired cannonballs over the Piazza del Santa Croce in Florence during a match, the players simply turned, flashed obscene gestures at the Prince, and continued to play.

Medieval peasants in France and England played ball games between villages particularly on Shrove Tuesday, the last day before the onset of Lent. At Derby, fueled by Shrovetide ale, the common folk from St Peter's and All Saints' parishes played a football game that stretched over three miles of countryside. The object was to kick, carry, or throw a ball to a waterwheel at All Saints' or a gate at St Peter's. There were few rules, so bites, scratches, and broken bones were common. It was a time to settle old scores of resentment between villagers. So disruptive were these events that in 1410 and 1414 on the eve of the Battle of Agincourt, Henry V ordered the people to practice archery rather than football. Edward IV banned football in 1477, and so did Henry VIII in 1496 to little avail. It was too embedded in folk custom and football games continued.

## Soccer and rugby

At Eton in the mid-nineteenth century the students played a "wall game" in which teams of 20 boys tried to shove and kick a ball along a 120-yard brick wall toward a small garden door at one end or a tree stump at the other. At Rugby School the boys had open space and so developed their game with kicking, running with the ball, pushing, hacking (kicking in the shins), and massive scrums (clumped struggles). Rugby published its rules in 1845, and in 1848 14 representatives of various English schools met to work out common laws so that they could play one another. An argument between Eton and Rugby about running with the ball resulted in the rejection of Rugby standards. Eton wrote its own rules in 1849 and outcast Rugby adopted an oval ball in 1851, a shape that would discourage kicking.

The festering argument was not ended until 1863 when the new Football Association in London banned tripping, hacking, holding, pushing, and carrying or throwing the ball. In speech, people shortened the awkward name "Football Association" to "Assoc," and then to "soccer." With the exception of the United States, it should be mentioned, elsewhere in the world soccer is also called "football." Meanwhile, the Rugby proponents said that football had been emasculated and left the London meetings in a huff.

Soccer thus emerged from a middle-class, schoolboy pastime rooted in a medieval peasant game. It was cheap to play and easy to understand. All that was needed was a ball, an open field, and goals. The purpose was to kick or head the ball into the goal without the use of hands. As rules evolved the game was played with 11 members per team, a field 120 yards long by 75–100 yards wide and two 45-minute halves. There were only 17 laws most of which dealt with penalties and fouls. Consequently, the game spread quickly as clubs formed in churches, factories, and towns. Newspapers took note of the competition and crowds became willing to pay to watch games. This, in turn, provided money to recruit and employ the best players.

In 1883 a team of Lancashire workmen called the Blackburn Olympic beat a team of gentlemen amateurs called the Old Etonians in an association championship. It was an important moment because no team of amateurs ever won the championship again. The Football League for professionals subsequently formed in 1885. The professionals attracted six million spectators during the 1905–1906 season and became the major source of male entertainment. Soccer thus became a "people's game" with strong links to the working class. Regardless of rule writing in the elite schools, in a sense football (soccer) had always been a game of the people.

More than at other sports contests the spectators at soccer games have proven unruly. Although there are instances of crowd violence at earlier periods, disruptions became a predictable phenomenon for soccer after 1960. In Lima, Peru 300 people were killed in a post-game riot in 1964; at Lenin Stadium in Moscow 340 people were trampled to death in 1982; at Sheffield, England 95 people were crushed against a fence during a stampede to get into the stadium in 1989; riots in the stands killed 39 in Brussels at the European championships in 1985; 20 fans died in 1987 in Tripoli trying to escape knife-wielding ruffians; at least 40 people died in brawling in 1991 during an exhibition match in Orkney, South Africa; during the championships in 2000, to prevent trouble, officials in Belgium arrested 464 English fans and sent them back to England.

Sociologist Eric Dunning has explained such "hooliganism" as originating among frustrated, lower-class males who enjoy the violence as a part of a crowd. The soccer game itself was secondary. Reporter Bill Buford in *Among the Thugs* (1990) confirmed this in a conversation with one of the British hooligans who told him, "The violence. We've all got it in us. It just needs a cause. It needs an acceptable way of coming out." For the cities and nations that host soccer matches the only solution to the riots has been crowd control, stadium modification such as the use of moats, and expulsion of known hooligans before they can cause trouble.

Meanwhile, the students at Rugby School stubbornly followed their own path of sports development. In 1871 the Rugby Football Union formed, allowing the handling of the ball, but outlawing the hacking that supported the old maxim, "You kick the ball if you can, and if you can't you kick the other man's shins." The size of teams was limited to 15, the venue remained about the size of a soccer field, and the union eventually set five as the number of points scored for carrying the ball past the end line and two for kicking it between the goal posts. In the 1880s new laws opened up the game with lateral passes and downfield running tactics. The organization retained tackles and the slugging, mauling, shoving scrum. Rugby remained a more aggressive and physical sport than soccer and kept its home largely in the schools of the middle and upper classes.

Dedicated players discouraged professionalism even to the point of excluding numbers on player's uniforms, and at a match where King George V complained that he could not identify participants, a Scottish official snapped, "This is a rugby match, not a cattle sale." In reaction to such rigidity and class discrimination the Northern Rugby Football Union (later the Rugby Football League) formed in 1895, and allowed "broken-time payments," or compensation for lost wages, so that working people could participate in the sport. A series of rule changes such as an orderly release of the ball after a tackle along with 13 players per side made rugby league a faster, more open game. This encouraged overseas migration of the sport to Australia and New Zealand in the early twentieth century.

## American football

Rugby directly allows creation of American football

Rugby had a direct influence on American football, a sport widely popular in the United States, but not elsewhere in the world. Similarities to rugby include an elongated oval ball, tackling, a large rectangular field, touchdowns (tries in rugby), and points through an "H" shaped goal post. Both are contact sports, but in America the players are extensively armored. The development of American football came about at the same time and emerged from the same sort of school atmosphere as rugby and soccer. The first games were intramural affrays between freshmen and sophomores in the eastern colleges, but in 1869 Rutgers and Princeton engaged in two football contests, one on each campus, that allowed 25 men per team to play a game much like soccer.

In 1874 McGill University of Montreal played two games against Harvard. The players changed the rules for each game, but the regulations were much like rugby. The following year Yale played against Harvard in a game that combined the laws of rugby and soccer. In 1876, to limit the confusion, Columbia, Harvard, Princeton, and Yale formed the Inter-collegiate Football Association (IFA) in order to schedule contests with each other and to codify the rules.

During the 1880s American football diverged from soccer and rugby through a series of rule changes inspired largely by Walter C. Camp (1859–1925) of Yale. He was a student-athlete at Yale from 1875–1882 and later served as the unpaid Yale coach and representative to the IFA. He worked in a nearby New Haven watch factory which may explain the extreme time fixation of the game. Starting in 1880 Camp suggested halting play anytime a player went down and allowing him to kick the ball back to a quarterback from a "line of scrimmage" (taken from the word "skirmish", a kind of battle). This was a "down" that stopped the action and constituted a major break with the constant flow of soccer and rugby. He obtained a reduction in team members from 15 to 11, later recommended that a team had to move the ball five yards in three downs (now ten yards in four downs) in order to retain possession, and tinkered with the scoring system of touchdowns, field goals, and extra points.

To keep track of the downs the field had to be marked and at first it was chalked in a gridiron fashion with straight lines both length and breadth. Eventually, the length lines were dropped in favor of "hash marks" as a point on the field to place the ball after it went out of bounds, but the term "gridiron" remained as a term for the football field. In the twentieth century the football stadium, large and small, became a landmark feature of the American urban landscape. In the 1920s and 1930s, for example, Yale built a concrete facility for 67,000 fans; Ohio State for 64,000; Los Angeles County with the 1932 Olympics in mind for 75,000; and Chicago with Soldier Field for professional football at 100,000. Large stadiums for football and baseball became a necessity for cities that desired a "big league" image.

As the sport spread through the colleges concern about injuries mounted. After 18 high school and college students died in 1905 President Theodore Roosevelt called a White House conference to discuss the problem, but nothing was accomplished. When Henry B. McCracken, the chancellor of New York University, lost a student in a game with Union College that same year, he called a conference of 62 colleges to reform the game and make it safer. The resultant organization at first named the Intercollegiate Athletic Association changed its title in 1910 to the National Collegiate Athletic Association (NCAA). It became the governing organization for American football, and subsequently for the remainder of collegiate sports.

The association banned interlocking interference whereby players locked arms as they ran down the field, and required seven offensive men to be placed on the line of scrimmage. This eliminated the use of the "flying wedge" tactic where offensive players formed a "V" and plowed over the defenders. With protective equipment such as helmets and shoulder pads the game became safer, more "civilized" in Dunning's terms. After the NCAA legalized the forward pass the ball itself changed from a fat oval like a rugby ball to an elongated oval that made it easier to throw.

Outstanding coaches such as Knute Rockne of Notre Dame, Glenn S. "Pop" Warner of Carlisle Institute and other places, Bernie Bierman of Minnesota, and Clark D. "Chuck" Shaughnessy of Stanford devised deceptive plays, but the most influential coach was Vincent T. Lombardi (1913–1970) of the professional Green Bay Packers. Professional football had blossomed with various weekend teams and in 1920 the owners organized the American Professional Football Association. It changed its name to the National Football League (NFL) two years later.

Following a learning career as an assistant coach Lombardi took over the losing Packers in 1959. He announced to the team at the first meeting, "I have never been on a losing team, gentlemen, and I don't intend to start now." He was a perfectionist who won five championships including the first two Super Bowls. The phrase, "Winning isn't everything, it's the only thing," has been attributed to Lombardi, perhaps inaccurately, but he did say, "Winning is not a sometime thing here, it is an all-the-time thing." The extreme emphasis upon winning and the denigration of losing has been a part of American sports ever since Lombardi.

Unable to obtain professional franchises from the NFL, oil millionaires Lamar Hunt of Dallas and K. S. "Bud" Adams of Houston formed the American Football League (AFL) in 1960. After a period of harsh war between the two leagues for players, prestige, and television coverage the two groups merged in 1967. This allowed for the first Super Bowl to be played between the champions of the leagues. Critics considered the AFL weak and unworthy until Super Bowl III when quarterback Joe Willie Namath of the New York Jets picked apart the Baltimore Colts with accurate passing and won 16–7. Before the game the confident Namath announced, "We're going to win. I guarantee it!" That ended much of the criticism of the AFL and the Super Bowl has gone on to become America's greatest sports extravaganza.

American football spread across the border to Canada with minor adjustments in the size of the playing field and numbers of players, but it has not attracted much participation outside North America. An obvious reason for this is cost—the sport yearly absorbs about 40 percent of major college athletic budgets—and its complexity. It has many more rules than soccer, involves intricate maneuvers on offense and defense, and emphasizes male strength and power. American football appears, for better or worse, to be a warrior game, a clash of virile gladiators with undertones of religious sanction.

A famous sportswriter, Grantland Rice (1880–1954) reported about the Notre Dame backfield after a game against the Army in 1924: "Outlined against a blue-gray October sky, the Four Horsemen rode again. In dramatic lore they are known as Famine, Pestilence, Destruction, and Death. These are only aliases. Their real names are Stuhldreyer, Miller, Crowley, and Layden." The names of the players have been long forgotten, but not the image of Notre Dame's Four Horsemen. The newsman's words reflected not only the common hyperbole of sports writing with a reference to the Four Horsemen of the Apocalypse, but also a linkage to religion. The quotation has been long remembered.

## Basketball and volleyball

If America contributed a uniquely violent game to the world with its brand of football, it also presented two gentler large-ball sports with basketball and volleyball. Unlike many modern sports that evolved from traditional roots, basketball and volleyball were actually invented by instructors for the Young Men's Christian Association (YMCA). The history of these sports cannot be divorced from that of the "Y" that began in London in 1844 as a social and religious refuge for young men. The thought was to provide a wholesome alternative for young men seeking to resist the temptations of urban life. In the nonsectarian YMCA buildings found throughout the world often there were dormitories, cafeterias, gymnasiums, swimming pools, and places to meet for classes or religious study. The YMCA purposely trained leaders for the new branches as they spread to world cities, and its logo, an equal sided triangle standing on a point, symbolized its purpose of serving mind, body, and spirit.

Luther H. Gulick (1865–1918) who directed physical education at the International YMCA Training School at Springfield, Massachusetts from 1887 to 1900 promoted the triangle symbol and also new sports for relief from the dull calisthenics of the gymnasiums. In 1891 Gulick asked James Naismith (1861–1939) one of his instructors, to devise an indoor ball game for use during the winter months. Working on the problem, Naismith, a Canadian with experience as the captain of the McGill rugby team, rejected the thought of running or tackling on a hardwood floor. He also thought that a goal located at ground level would be too easy, but that an elevated box of some sort that would require a soft, arched throw might work.

For that purpose a janitor found some wooden peach baskets and nailed them to a railing about ten feet above the floor. Naismith wrote down rules for players to pass the ball and try to shoot it into the basket. Using a soccer ball he divided his somewhat reluctant class into nine men per team and launched the new game of "basket ball." The janitor had to use a ladder to retrieve the ball whenever it went into the peach basket so there had to be adjustments in the techniques of the game.

Eventually, basketball utilized 20-minute halves, 1-point free throws for fouls, dribbling to allow running with the ball, a field goal that counted two points, a standard size ball, teams of five players, sturdy backboards, and a hoop with nets that allowed the ball to fall through. It was intended to be a non-contact sport. The YMCA along with other athletic organizations fine-tuned the rules in the early twentieth century, but the purpose of the game—to score the most points by shooting the ball through the basket—was easily understood by people throughout the world. The YMCA publicized the game in the newsletters of its global system and the new sport shortly migrated to the schools as well. By 1895 basketball was being played not only in the United States and Canada, but also in England, France, China, and India. Considering the number of both participants and fans basketball enthusiasts claim it to be the most popular sport in the world.

Volleyball followed a similar path of creation and dispersion. William G. Morgan, one of Naismith's students who became the physical education director of the Holyoke, Massachusetts YMCA, wanted a pleasant, mild, non-contact game for middle-aged businessmen who found basketball too strenuous. In 1895 he devised a game whereby teams of men batted with their hands a large ball back and forth over a net placed slightly above their heads. He modeled the game after badminton and put on a demonstration at a Springfield meeting in 1896.

In time, rule adjustments called for 6 players per team, a net placed at almost 8 feet, points scored only by the serving team, and matches of the best of 5 sets of 25 points per set. The A. G. Spalding Company created a lightweight ball to accommodate the new game. Like basketball, volleyball was easy to understand, cheap, and entertaining. And like basketball the new game spread instantly through the global YMCA network.

## Swimming

In this same time frame of the last part of the nineteenth century other modern sports also developed. Swimming, track and field, wrestling, fencing, skiing, and boxing emerged as organized sports. Swimming had been noted in ancient Egypt and Greece—Pausanias wrote that races were held in honor of the god, Dionysus. A book on the art of swimming by Everard Digby appeared in England in 1587, and it was taught in Japanese schools at the end of the Tokugawa era. Pools opened in Liverpool, England as early as 1828 and in 1837 London had six pools that hosted competitions. In 1869 the Metropolitan Swimming Club Association held a one-mile championship down the Thames River between Putney Aqueduct and Hammersmith Bridge. Sydney, Australia staged open water contests in 1846. The Dolphin Swim Club of Toronto, Canada formed in 1876 and held a championship for seven swimmers one year later. The New York Athletic Club began a US national championship in 1877. By 1910 the YMCA possessed 293 pools in the United States and embarked on a "Teaching America to Swim" campaign to instruct the populace about this life-saving skill. Thus, interest in the sport evolved.

Early racers mainly used breaststroke—as was utilized by Matthew Webb (1848–1883) in the first swim across the English Channel in 1875. In 1873, however, John Arthur Trudgen introduced an alternating, over-arm stroke combined with a scissors kick that he had seen used in South Africa. The Australian crawl with an over-arm stroke and an up and down kick replaced the Trudgen stroke for speed after being introduced in England by Richard Cavill in 1902. His father who taught swimming in Sydney had observed the stroke in the Solomon Islands and taught it to his children. Then, Americans synchronized a six-beat flutter kick from Hawaii with the over-arm stroke to perfect the American crawl which in turn became the fastest of the racing strokes. Gertrude Ederle (1906–2003) of New York City used it in 1926 to best the men's time for swimming the English Channel by over two hours, and Johnny Weissmuller (1904–1984) of the Illinois Athletic Club in Chicago used the American crawl to break every swimming record up to 880 yards. His record of 51 seconds for 100 yards set in 1927 was not surpassed until 1943. Tall, broad-chested and handsome, Weissmuller used his athletic prowess in 19 Tarzan movies to become one of the earliest international sports stars.

## Skiing and ice hockey

Like swimming, skiing has a long tradition, but in the cold countries that reach from the Baltic to Asia. Skis have been found in northern Russian and Scandinavian bogs that are 4,000 years old and there is mention of cross-country contests in the Norse sagas. Norwegian ski troops, however, participated in the first modern competition in 1787 for monetary prizes awarded for shooting while skiing, bushwhacking, downhill racing, and for running with full equipment. The military unit disbanded in 1826, but local civilian clubs took up the sport and organized contests. In the last half of the nineteenth century Scandinavians emigrated throughout the world and took their skis to Australia and to the Americas where they were used for traveling and winter recreation.

Nordic skiing, which included cross-country and jumping, along with Alpine, or downhill, skiing became a wealthy person's sport in Europe by 1900 and the Norwegians called an international conference in 1910 to establish rules. The Federation Internationale de Ski (FIS) subsequently took control in 1924 to become the world governing body for skiing competition. Acrobatic, or freestyle skiing had been a part of professional ski shows since 1900, but did not achieve inclusion with competitive skiing until the 1970s. Snowboards produced first in 1966 for "snurfers," or snow surfers, became so popular that they now rival skis for recreation and became accepted for events in the Winter Olympics in 1998.

By the 1920s most of the mountainous areas of Europe recognized the opportunity of winter tourism and built ski resorts. The United States, slow to grasp the commercial opportunity, nonetheless constructed a resort, Timberline Lodge, near Portland, Oregon as a depression relief project. The industry boomed after World War II when ski troopers returned home and pursued their skiing skills as recreation in the Rocky Mountain West.

Members of the tenth Mountain Division who had trained in Colorado, for example, returned to reshape the old mining village of Aspen, Colorado into a ski town.

Ice hockey, also a cold weather sport, came about when medieval Europeans, adapting ice skates that had been in use for some 2,000 years, tried their stick and ball games on frozen ponds and canals. The modern version came in 1875 when J. G. A. Creighton (1850–1930) and other young men combined the rules of rugby, lacrosse, polo, and shinty for a game on the indoor Victoria Rink in Montreal, Canada. The rules evolved: numbers of players per team went from nine to seven; the puck changed from a rubber ball to a block of wood to a hard rubber disk; face-offs were introduced to start or renew play; tripping and holding were identified as fouls.

By the 1890s dozens of teams thrived in Eastern Canada and the Governor General of Canada, Lord Preston of Stanley (1841–1908) donated a cup for the best team in the dominion. Playoffs between leagues attracted thousands of spectators and top teams began to pay talented players with cash and employment. The openly professional teams that appeared across Canada in the early twentieth century eventually formed the National Hockey League in 1917. Meanwhile, ice hockey became popular with male participants in Great Britain, Europe, and among college students in the Eastern United States. In the late 1920s professional ice hockey spread into the Northeastern United States and amateur hockey became a part of the Winter Olympics. Climate and lack of resources have restricted the diffusion of ice hockey and consequently, the sport is but sparsely supported in Asia, the Middle East, Africa, and South America.

## Running and throwing

Interest in running and throwing, like swimming and skiing, persisted from ancient times into the modern period. In China, for example, running was valued as a military skill and in the Yuan Dynasty (1271–1368) imperial guards were expected to be able to run 90 kilometers in 6 hours. The Highland Games of Scotland, another example, harked back to clan gatherings for military purposes and placed emphasis upon speed and strength. The Scots threw river stones, hammers, and cabers. Suppressed after the Battle of Culloden (1746) the games revived in the early nineteenth century as community celebrations. In 1822 the meeting at Inverness included an eight-mile foot race, and the Braemar Games in 1837 featured hammer throws, a stone put, a hop-skip-leap, and sprint runs. In 1848 Queen Victoria visited the ongoing Braemar Games and made them fashionable. Immigrating Scots of the nineteenth century took these Highland Games with them wherever they moved, and they were a restless people.

In the United States 14 track and field enthusiasts established the New York Athletic Club (NYAC) in 1868 and built a clubhouse at the Elysian Fields, a portion of the John Cox Steven's estate at Hoboken set aside for the athletic clubs of the New York City aristocracy. The NYAC hosted the first national championships in track and field in 1876, for swimming in 1877, and for boxing, fencing, and wrestling in 1878.

## Amateurism

The club accepted from England the idea of the amateur athlete, a person who did not compete for money or make a living instructing in a sport. This drew a line between an amateur who competed for the love of a sport, and the professional who made money from athletic activity. As expressed by Walter C. Camp: "A gentleman does not make his living from his athletic prowess. He does not earn anything from his victories except glory and satisfaction."

It was a pernicious concept that discriminated against the lower class and constricted athletic progress until given up in the latter part of the twentieth century. The NYAC willingly yielded its nascent control over these individual sports to the National Association of Amateur Athletes of America in 1879 that in turn surrendered its rule to the Amateur Athletic Union (AAU) in 1888. By the end of the century the AAU controlled 250,000 athletes bound to the amateur code.

## Professionalism and boxing

Professionalism, in contrast, flourished with boxing from its early beginnings at the ancient Olympic Games. People were willing to pay to see a good fight and to have the opportunity to gamble. In London James Figg opened a school to teach the "manly art of self-defense" in the early eighteenth century. He taught gentlemen to fight with swords, cudgels, and fists for their personal defense, and built a demonstration hall with room for several hundred spectators to sit around a raised circular stage called "the ring." In 1727 Figg took on a personal challenger, Ned Sutton who was a pipemaker from Greenwich. King George I joined the gambling crowd to watch as Figg opened a cut on Sutton's shoulder with a sword, knocked him down with his fists, and shattered his knee with a cudgel. Figg retired as a rich man at age 36.

Prizefights between women wearing tight jackets, short petticoats, white stockings, and pumps also took place at Figg's ring and elsewhere. With their husbands women fought other couples with swords and quarter-staffs (cudgels) for prizes of £40 or higher. Information is slight, but Mrs. Stokes, the "City Championess," fought the Hibernian Heroine at the amphitheater, and in 1768 "Bruising Peg" triumphed over an outclassed opponent.

Jack Broughton, a Figg student, took over the teaching and became the best boxer in England. During a grueling match in 1741 Broughton hit his opponent below the heart and killed him. Upset, Broughton devised a set of rules to lessen the brutality: no wrestling, no hitting below the belt, no hitting a man who was down, a 30-second rest after a knockdown. The rules introduced the idea of rounds, but the rounds were neither periodic nor limited in number. Fights lasted until a participant could no longer "come up to scratch," a line in the center of the ring, and gloves were used only in practice. After losing a heavily wagered match when he was 46 years old, Broughton retired. His rules persisted and at his death in 1789 he was honored with burial in the courtyard of Westminster Abbey in the company of famous politicians, soldiers, and writers.

In one of the earliest transnational events, Tom Molineaux, a black man who supposedly had fought his way out of slavery, left New York in 1810 to challenge the leading English fighter, Tom Cribb. In the twenty-ninth round Cribb closed one of Molineaux's eyes, and in the thirty-ninth round the American black fell from exhaustion. The fight continued until the forty-fourth round when Cribb knocked out Molineaux. In a return match in 1811 before a crowd of 40,000 fans Cribb broke Molineaux's jaw in the tenth round and knocked him out in the eleventh. Cribb used his winnings to start a successful pub that still exists in the heart of London; Molineaux drifted into the backcountry, gave boxing demonstrations, and died penniless in Galway, Ireland in 1818.

In another cross-Atlantic bout in 1860 John C. Heenan, the American champion fought Tom Sayers outside of London. British aristocrats joined riffraff to witness a 2-hour, 20-minute bloodbath. Heenan was six feet one inch tall and weighed 190 pounds. Sayers was five feet eight inches tall and weighed 160 pounds. In the seventh round Sayers lost the use of his right arm with either a pulled muscle or broken bone, but continued to fight. Finally, with both men bloody and exhausted, and the crowd out of control the referee called the fight a draw.

To "civilize" boxing after this bloodbath, Sir John Sholto Douglas, the eighth Marquis of Queensberry proposed the so-called Queensberry Rules in 1867 that established three-minute rounds with a one-minute rest, a ten-second knockout, three weight classes, the use of gloves, and a prohibition of blows to the kidney, back of the neck, or below the belt. There was no limit to the number of rounds for professionals; amateurs usually fought for only three rounds.

The championship fight between John L. Sullivan (1858–1918), the "Boston Strong Boy," and "Gentleman Jim" Corbett in 1892 in New Orleans established the use of the Queensberry Rules in the United States.

Sullivan who had fought most of his bouts with bare fists was out of condition and lost in the twenty-first round, so tired that he could not raise his arms. He, nonetheless, gave a gracious speech to the ringside crowd after the fight, retired from the sport, and went on to a career as a popular temperance (anti-liquor) speaker. The outgoing Sullivan had toured the country giving demonstrations and received extensive publicity in the cheap popular newspapers that emerged in the last part of the nineteenth century. He was America's first national sports hero.

Sullivan like many other white fighters avoided bouts with blacks. Jack Johnson (1878–1946), a black who had grown up on the docks of Galveston, Texas, however, found a way to win the heavyweight championship. Johnson pursued the reigning champion, Tommy Burns, around the world and finally cornered him into a fight in Australia in 1908. Johnson won easily and shocked the racist United States with a flashy lifestyle that included fast cars and white women. To avoid a prison sentence for taking a woman across state lines for immoral purposes, Johnson fled the United States in 1913 to live in Europe. He was caught by World War I in 1914, ran out of money, and agreed to fight Jess Willard (a "white hope") in Cuba in 1915. There, Johnson lost in the twenty-sixth round. After wandering about Mexico he returned to the United States in 1920, served a one-year prison term, and spent the rest of his life giving boxing exhibitions.

After a period of fine white boxers such as Jack Dempsey and the first major fight promotions by George L. "Tex" Rickard, another black, Joe Louis, became champion in 1937. Like Jack Johnson, Joe Louis (1914–1981) grew up poor, but learned to box in Detroit and gave his mother his first prize of $59. He avoided the racial animosity directed toward Jack Johnson by remaining humble in public and by knocking out Max Schmeling, the German champion, in 1938. Europe was about to boil over into World War II and even though he did not consider himself a Nazi, Schmeling was looked upon as a representative of the Third Reich by both Hitler and the press. In 1936 Louis had lost to Schmeling, but in a 1938 return match Louis knocked him out in the first round. Louis, the "Brown Bomber" defended his title a record 25 times in 12 years, served in World War II, retired undefeated, failed in a comeback, and fell into such tax debt that he had to be rescued by a special act of Congress. At death, however, he was honored with burial in Arlington National Cemetery, the Valhalla of America's war heroes.

Although he did not achieve as good a record as Louis (70 professional fights, 67 wins, 53 knockouts) the most flamboyant modern boxer was Muhammad Ali (61 professional fights, 56 wins, 37 knockouts). He won the light-heavyweight division in the 1960 Olympics, turned to professional fighting, and took the heavyweight championship from Sonny Liston in 1964. At the same time he joined the Nation of Islam, the Black Muslims, and changed his name from Cassius Clay to Muhammad Ali to the surprise of the country. In 1967 he refused induction into the United States Army for the war in Vietnam. "I ain't got no quarrels with them Viet Congs," he said as he was sentenced to five years in prison.

His lawyers kept him out of jail, however, and Ali became a popular anti-war spokesman while he awaited the return of his licenses to box. The Supreme Court set aside his sentence in 1971 as Ali resumed his career after a three-year absence from the sport. He then fought epic battles with Joe Frazier, George Foreman, Leon Spinks and others before he retired in 1981 already showing permanent brain damage from his life in the ring. Ali became a symbol of black pride and for resistance to an unpopular war. He became so well known around the world for his scheduled fights in Zaire and the Philippines, his knack for publicity, and his skill that Ali might well be considered the first international sports hero. Few people have forgotten his pronouncement of "I'm the greatest!" and his mantra, "Float like a butterfly, sting like a bee."

## Auto racing

The professionalism that dominated boxing diminished the popularity of amateurs. The same is true of another sport that expresses more than any other the technological capacity of humanity—automobile racing. It is common lore that the first auto race was predestined as soon as the second car was built. Manufacturers wanted to prove that they produced the fastest and most durable vehicle, and so racing started soon after invention occurred. A race took place, for example, between Paris and Rouen in 1894 followed by another from Paris to Bordeaux and back in 1895. It was won by a French car that averaged 15 miles per hour. A Grand Prix event was held at Le Mans in 1906 for 32 entrants that required 12 laps of a 100-kilometer circuit. Eleven cars finished and Ferenc Szisz won with a Renault averaging 63 miles per hour.

Henry Ford built the first racecar in America and he hired Barney Oldfield, a champion bicycle competitor, to drive it to a world speed record of 91 miles per hour in 1904. The Automobile Club of America that later became the American Automobile Association (AAA) sponsored a Thanksgiving Day race at Savannah in 1908 and a crowd of 200,000 showed up to watch. This provided a glimpse of the spectator interest in the new sport and the AAA continued to sponsor races until 1955 when it withdrew because of bad publicity from fatalities.

In 1909 the Indianapolis Motor Speedway opened and in 1911 it was paved with brick. The first Memorial Day 500-mile race (200 laps) was held in 1911 at "the brickyard" and Ray Harroun won with an average speed of 75 miles per hour. The first cars carried the driver and a mechanic. In the

1930s, low-slung single-seat cars regularly began to average over 100 miles per hour. In 1961 Jack Brabham from Australia drove a rear-engined Cooper-Climax to ninth place and started a shift to cars with the engine mounted in the rear. Ari Luyendyk of Arizona set the track record of an average 186 miles per hour in 1990.

Grand Prix competitions in Europe halted during World War I, revived between the wars, stopped once more during World War II, and began again after the war. The first race cars were mainly modified passenger vehicles, but from 1920 to 1950 they became streamlined, front-engine, rear-drive roadsters. The first Formula 1 championship took place in 1950. Since 1960 these open-wheeled racecars have been designed with the engine located behind the driver and in front of the rear wheels. In the 1970s manufacturers produced a wedge-shaped body with front and rear airfoils to increase downward air pressure to improve cornering.

Racing rules and car specifications meant to ensure safety for drivers, crews, and spectators have been set and adjusted frequently by the Federation Internationale de l'Automobile (FIA) since its establishment in 1904. During the 1980s, for example, manufacturers introduced turbo-charged engines so powerful that the FIA banned them in 1989. Current regulations, interestingly, also ban four-wheel drive, traction control, and antilock brakes, features that are considered safety features for normal road cars. The reason was to put emphasis upon driver skill.

Formula 1 cars are enormously expensive—Ferrari's race budget in 1999 was $240 million—and the races around irregular courses or city streets are dangerous. Since 1950, 24 drivers have died. In the last half of the twentieth century Great Britain has provided the most successful drivers, but the drivers Michael Schumacher of Germany, Juan-Manuel Fangio of Argentina, and Alain Prost of France own the greatest number of world championships. Schumacher, who earned $59 million in 2000 for his Formula 1 championship, ranked ahead of Tiger Woods ($53 million) and Michael Jordan ($37 million) as the most highly paid sportsman. The sport has been strongly supported by the media in Europe and Formula 1 racing boasts 350 million television viewers in 150 countries. Only the Olympics attracts higher viewer ratings.

Other motorized sports have likewise evolved such as drag racing and motorcycle sports, but stock car racing seems to have caught recent popular interest in the United States. It appeals to a fantasy of competing with the family car against rush hour traffic at 150 miles per hour. The National Association for Stock Car Auto Racing (NASCAR) led by William H. G. "Bill" France began in 1947 for the promotion of races between supposedly everyday cars from the streets.

The first race—150 miles on a dirt oval at Charlotte, North Carolina in 1949 for $5,000—was open to all drivers with a full-sized American car.

Some 31 racers in nine different makes of automobiles showed up. The most memorable moment of the race came when Lee Petty, father of Richard Petty who later won 1,185 professional races, tumbled his new family Buick end over end to land on its wheels. Petty got out of the wreck, sat on the edge of the track, and told a passerby who asked, "I was just sitting here thinking about having to go home and explain to my wife where I'd been with the car."

Glenn Dunnaway won the race, but was disqualified when officials found that he was driving a "bootlegger" car with modified rear springs that allowed him to take the turns faster than normal. NASCAR, still run by the France family, now schedules circuit races of high-powered closed wheeled cars costing $60,000 to $120,000 on large paved tracks that attract up to 100,000–200,000 spectators per event. Race rules and consciously designed safety features such as roll cages, rubberized fuel tanks, and padded track walls have civilized the sport so that there can be spectacular crashes from which the driver usually walks away—thrills without the blood.

## Sports organizations

Most of the world sports in their modern context as characterized by historian Allen Guttmann seemed to assume identity during the last half of the nineteenth century to the early part of the twentieth century, about a 60-year span. At least, this was the time when governing bodies were established to set schedules, fix rules, and hold championships. There are some exceptions—horse racing, cricket, and golf—but the founding of most modern sports organizations appears to cluster in that period. With the ongoing rational organization of big corporations in the West it might be expected that bureaucratic principles would spill over into the formation of sports governing bodies. The educated, managerial classes in most cases ran the initial sports groups as well as the businesses so their skills could easily transfer from one realm to another.

## Conclusion

The nineteenth century was a time of expanding wealth, maturing industrialization, urbanization, and overseas extension in trade and military power for the West. It was a time too of confusion as the rural population shifted into the cities and people searched for order and purpose in their lives. There remained all the earlier motives for sport such as warfare, religion, and eros, but the forces of modernization gave definition to modern sports. Compact populations provided opportunity for athletes to find competition and for promoters to stage contests. This led to the building of stadiums and professionalism.

Although sociologists have studied recent soccer hooliganism the distant history of spectators has been generally ignored with many questions about class, place, and gender left unanswered. It would seem, nevertheless, that fans have always experienced some level of pleasurable recreation and emotional involvement. Otherwise, why bother with a sporting event? At a time of tedious factory or office work, however, a boxing match, horse race, baseball game, or running contest was memorable. It was something to talk about, a diversion from the everyday pattern, an enrichment of life. Athletic contests became a major source of socially acceptable recreation and the bans of Puritanism no longer held in the secular circumstance of the city. Modern sport therefore was a product of its times, and a cultural reflection of its times.

## Further reading

For general information about sports: David Levinson and Karen Christensen (eds), *Encyclopedia of World Sport* (Santa Barbara, California: ABC-CLIO, 1996), 3 vols.; William J. Baker, *Sports in the Western World* (Urbana: University of Illinois, 1988); Maarten Van Bottenburg, *Global Games* (Urbana: Illinois, 2001); Norbert Elias and Eric Dunning, *Quest for Excitement: Sport and Leisure in the Civilizing Process* (New York: Basil Blackwell, 1986); Ralph Hickok, *The Encyclopedia of North American Sports History* (New York: Facts on File, 1992); David G. McComb, *Sports: An Illustrated History* (New York: Oxford, 1998). See also: Bill Buford, *Among the Thugs* (New York: Vintage Books, 1990); Allen Guttmann, *Sports Spectators* (New York: Columbia, 1986); Richard Holt, *Sport and the British* (New York: Oxford, 1990); Howard G. Knuttgen, Ma Qiwei, and Wu Zhongyuan (eds), *Sport in China* (Champaign, Illinois: Human Kinetics, 1990; Hans Westerbeek and Aaron Smith, *Sport Business in the Global Marketplace* (New York: Palgrave Macmillan, 2003).

# Chapter 4

# The Globalization of Sport

Modern sports spread throughout the world from the West as a result of individual enthusiasm, Christian missionary work, sport governing groups, military occupation, and the Olympic Games. These elements make up the main topics of this chapter. Sports were a part of the cultural baggage carried by Westerners abroad in their quest for empire, trade, and influence. Their ideas about sports were transferred both with deliberation and by casual circumstance to others who adapted and emulated the habits of the foreigners. It was not all one-way, and some sports such as polo and judo, after acquiring the attributes of modern Western sports, found their way into the global sports network.

There has been a high degree of standardization because as the nineteenth century sports groups discovered, if there was to be fair competition between teams, schools, individuals, or nations there must be an agreement about rules. Thus, international governing bodies with their bureaucracies, ambitions, records, regulations, and championships arose to enforce the same rules for everyone. And consequently, homogenization occurred. By far the most important organization has been the International Olympic Committee which projected global modern sports for the Olympic Games. With the agreements to conform on such items as standard distances in events, legal moves, length of contests, and acceptable equipment came also the hope for equality for all competitors. That has been the great promise of international sport.

## Enthusiasts and baseball

After Alexander Cartwright established baseball in New York City in 1845 he moved to Hawaii in 1849. As the "New York Game" caught hold in the United States Cartwright in 1852 enthusiastically laid out a diamond and proceeded to teach the islanders to play the game. In 1873, advocate Horace Wilson, an American teacher at Tokyo University, demonstrated baseball to his students, and in 1882 Hiroshi Hiraoka, a Japanese engineer who had studied in Boston and who became a Red Sox fan, established the first team in his homeland. Overseas Americans who played baseball at their exclusive Yokohama Athletic Club and who thought that only Americans were capable of playing "America's pastime," resisted competing with the Japanese. After five years of asking, however, they accepted a game with the Ichiko prep school in 1896. Answering a polite inquiry about the condition of the field because of bad weather, the foreigners sent a haughty telegram, "Are you trying to flee from us?"

In the game the Japanese boys fumbled about at first and then won 29–4. The members of the Japanese team became immediate national heroes, greeted with *banzai* cheers on the streets and celebratory cups of *sake* at home. They had beaten the Americans at their own game. At a time when Japan was trying to modernize its country the victory was taken as a sign that Japan had caught up with the West. The humiliated Americans played two more return games and lost 32-9 and 22-6. Finally, on 4 July 1896 with reinforcements from the *USS Olympia*, a battleship that had steamed into port, the Americans won 14-12. Baseball had come to Japan and had become a Japanese game.

Other Japanese school teams formed and like the Ichiko players took the game very seriously. Coach Suishu Tobita of the Waseda School commented, "If the players do not try so hard as to vomit blood in practice then they can not hope to win games. One must suffer to be good." In 1925 his squad defeated a touring University of Chicago team three times in a four-game series. Japan abandoned the foreign game during World War II, but revived it afterwards with youth teams and the establishment of a professional league in 1948. Counting television viewers, baseball became the most popular spectator sport in Japan as well as the most popular participant sport.

Toward the end of the twentieth century a handful of not altogether welcome American professionals played for Japanese teams, and a few Japanese players jumped to the major leagues in the United States. Randy Bass, for example, who had played for the San Diego Padres led the Hanshin Tigers of Japan to a series victory in 1985. When his home run total threatened the record of Japanese star Oh Sadaharu, however, pitchers repeatedly walked Bass to first base. On the other hand, pitcher Hideo Nomo began playing for the Los Angeles Dodgers in 1995, without difficulty followed by others such as Ichiro Suzuki with the Seattle Mariners, Tsuyoshi Shinjo with the New York Mets, and Hideki Matsui with the New York Yankees. This exchange was another step toward the globalization of the sport, and perhaps to a true "world series" of the future.

Baseball also spread through the Caribbean especially to Cuba, Mexico, Puerto Rico, and the Dominican Republic where it became more popular than soccer. Upper-class students from Cuba returned with the game in the

1860s and leagues formed in the 1870s. Nemesio Guillot in 1866, for example, brought both equipment and enthusiasm for the game home to Cuba in 1866 with the result that the professional Habana Baseball Club (1872), the Matanzas Club (1873), and the Almandares Club (1878) formed a league in 1878.

The Philadelphia Athletics toured the island in 1886 and baseball became the sport of the rebels who rejected bullfighting to protest Spanish rule. Spanish administrators tried to suppress baseball, but defeat in the Spanish-American War (1898) ended their effort. During the early twentieth century white and black Americans lured by the easy money of the Cuban owners traveled to Cuba to play "winter ball" in the off season. Baseball thus became the major sport of Cubans and a sport that has endured during the long isolation of the communist Castro regime (1959–). Dictator Fidel Castro, who learned to love the game while a student in the United States has remained a baseball enthusiast.

Cubans who fled their country when civil war broke out in 1868 introduced baseball to the Dominican Republic where it became popular with workers at the sugar refineries. It replaced cricket by the 1930s. David Arellano, a returning student from Grenada, Nicaragua, planted baseball in 1891 in his hometown as did other students in their towns. It became the most widely played sport in the early 1900's and amateur league play began in Managua in 1911–1912. United States Marine occupation of the country from 1912–1933 kept interest going by supplying officials and competition for local teams. In Puerto Rico an initial game was played in 1896, and US soldiers who occupied the island after the Spanish-American War popularized the sport.

Along the US-Mexican border American construction workers and military personnel played baseball for recreation in the 1880s and the sport reached Mexico City in 1884. American expatriates played amateur games at fiesta times and in 1904 a Mexican Baseball Association formed that was able to make $400 per game in receipts. American and Cuban professional teams toured the countryside and a summertime professional league started in 1925 when there were more than 150 amateur teams in the capital.

Latin American owners offered black players $775 with all expenses for an eight-week season which was more than could be made in the United States. The blacks competed as equals with whites on the field and were treated as equals away from the field. Willie Wells, leaving the Newark Eagles for Mexico in the 1930s explained:

> I've found freedom and democracy here, something I never found in the United States. I was branded a Negro in the United States and had to act accordingly. Everything I did, including playing ball was regulated by my color. Well, here . . . I am a man.

Until Jackie Robinson broke the color line in the United States only light-complexioned Latin American players could make it to the major leagues. For instance, on a junket to Cuba in 1911 the second-place World Series team, the New York Giants, lost their first two games. Jose Mendez, a dark, young, fireball pitcher for the Almendares Club outperformed star pitcher Christy Mathewson, but Mendez could never make it to the major leagues. "The Black Diamond," however, did play and led the Negro Kansas City Monarchs to a championship in 1924. Once the barrier was down Latin American players came to prominence in major league play—such as Roberto Clemente of Puerto Rico, Juan Marichal of the Dominican Republic, Luis Aparicio of Venezuela, Rafael Palmeiro of Cuba, and Sammy Sosa of the Dominican Republic. In the 2000 major league season about 20 percent of the players were Latin Americans.

Not only did individual players display their talents abroad, teams traveled on "missionary" tours to interest others in baseball. A. G. Spalding, baseball player, owner, and sports equipment entrepreneur, took demonstration teams to England in 1874 and 20 players around the world in 1888–1889. In Australia Spalding was careful to present baseball as a winter sport, not as a substitute for cricket. The players also performed in Hawaii, New Zealand, Egypt, Italy, France, and England before returning home. The impact was slight, but the Australians produced a team called the "Kangaroos" that toured the United States in 1897, played poorly, and went on to London where the manager abandoned the team and left the players holding an unpaid hotel bill. This discouraged baseball in Australia until World War II when American servicemen revived interest.

Baseball, however, has had a limited geographic spread—North America, the Caribbean, Philippines, and Japan. The best explanation offered for the limit is that it reflects the extent of American influence in educational and cultural matters. Also, baseball was already a fully developed "people's game" that traveling American soldiers, sailors, teachers, businessmen, and missionaries could easily carry with them. The geographic limit, therefore, reflects a boundary line of American influence. There is also the additional consideration that people liked the game. In Cuba it was embraced as a sport to oppose Spanish rule and gain independence, in Japan it represented the same idea, a reach for modernity. Baseball appeared in those places at the right time for ready acceptance by the populace. It was also fun and not imposed as cultural imperialism.

Victor Heiser, an American physician in the Philippines during the early military occupation of the islands after the Spanish-American War, for example, witnessed a successful substitution of baseball for headhunting among remote Igorot Indians. In *An American Doctor's Odyssey* (1936), he wrote:

I made many solitary trips into the Igorot country, usually forewarned by anxious friends that I would certainly be killed, because I could not tell when the savages would turn upon me. I was going along one day in a remote part of the country when my ears were startled by the most stupendous uproar of yelling and shouting. It sounded ominous, but there was no help for it. I had to go on. . . . The din increased as I proceeded. Suddenly I emerged into a clearing, but instead of spears and *bolos*, my eyes were startled with the sight of bats and balls, and the fantastic picture of a savage, naked save for a string around his middle and a great wire catcher's mask before his face. An inter-village baseball game was in progress. Nobody paid any attention to me; nobody knew or cared whether I had arrived. The teams were fairly matched, and I was soon raised to almost the same pitch of excitement. With one man on first base, a young Igorot came to bat and, with a resounding crack, hit the ball into left field. The man on first started for second, but it seemed almost certain he would be put out. With one accord the cry arose from the throats of the wild men, "Slide, you son of a bitch, slide!" The Igorots had watched the games of the American soldiers at the hill station, and were letter perfect in their lines.

## The diffusion of cricket

As baseball flourished under the umbrella of American global influence, cricket diffused within the British Empire. As historian Allen Guttmann wrote in his book *Games and Empires* (1994), "From the remnants of wickets and bats, future archaeologists of material culture will be able to reconstruct the boundaries of the British Empire." An International Cricket Conference started in 1909 with three members (England, Australia, and South Africa), added additional nations, changed its name to the International Cricket Council in 1989, separated from the Marylebone Cricket Club, and became the world governing body in 1993. Probably because of its complexity and its reputation as an elite sport, however, cricket did not attain the global acceptance of soccer. Moreover, as the British Empire dissolved, the popularity of cricket declined.

In Australia, however, people played cricket with little class or gender distinction. Military garrisons formed clubs in Sydney in 1826 followed by Melbourne and Adelaide. It became a part of school curriculums and international competition began with England. In 1873–1874 the great English player W. G. Grace toured Australia with a team and left behind two members to coach in Sydney and Melbourne. An Australian team beat the Marylebone Cricket Club at Lord's in 1878 and again in 1882. It was a delicious victory for the Aussies. It was memorable to beat the mother country and victory at cricket became a rite of passage toward home rule.

Australia was the first colony to beat England at cricket and it became independent in 1901.

The London *Sporting Times* jokingly lamented the death of English cricket and in an obituary said that the body would be cremated and sent to Australia. A group of Melbourne women subsequently burned a bail, put the ashes in an urn, and gave it to an English cricket captain. This started a bi-annual cricket contest to win the "Ashes," a dual contest still famous in both countries.

For the most part the matches were friendly, but in 1932–1933 the MCC sent a team captained by Douglas R. Jardine who believed in trying to intimidate batsmen. Jardine and others hurled sharply bouncing bowls aimed at the upper body and head rather than the wicket. When the batter protected himself with the bat the weakly hit ball could be easily fielded. Following Jardine's appointment as captain an observer wrote, "Well, we shall win the Ashes—but we may lose a Dominion." After two Australian batsmen were injured by straight-thrown balls the newspapers complained about the lack of sportsmanship in the "bodyline assault." The Australian Cricket Board cabled a complaint to London and the MCC, in turn, became insulted. No colonial should have the audacity to question the almighty MCC! Diplomats had to settle the matter. The world was in the Great Depression and the unity of empire was more important than cricket.

In spite of the growing popularity of baseball in the Caribbean, cricket was the sport of the elite of the British West Indies. Not only was it satisfying to beat the mother country at her own game, but also, cricket provided a chance for racial integration. All-white clubs recruited talented black players, and in 1960 Frank Worrell, a black man, was elected captain to lead the all-star West Indian team against the English and Australians. Worrell, educated in England, led successful tours to Australia in 1961 and to England in 1963. He was knighted in 1964 and buried in Westminster Abbey after his death from leukemia in 1966. Novelist V. S. Naipaul who was born in Trinidad noted that the cricket pitch with its laws of fair play provided a place where skill regardless of race was recognized. In time, cricket thus provided a door for racial and "colonial" acceptance.

The employees of the British East India Company practiced exclusion when it began playing cricket in India in 1721. Other British clubs likewise practiced discrimination. The Parsees, an upper-class Indian religious group in Bombay, nevertheless, formed a team in 1848. Lord Harris (George Robert Channing Harris, 1851–1932) who was viceroy to India at the end of the nineteenth century actually encouraged Indian play and started a tournament between the Parsees and British residents in 1892. To the shock of the local British population, Lord Harris, who later became the head of the Marylebone Cricket Club, actually sat down to lunch with the Indian athletes. "The game of cricket," he said, "has done more to draw the Mother

Country and the Colonies together than years of beneficial legislation could have done."

Upper-class Indians educated in England returned with enthusiasm for the game. It appealed to Indian royalty because of its aristocratic history, association with British rule, and the need for only light exertion in a hot climate. The most famous of these returning students was Prince Ranjitsinhji, Maharaja Jam Sahib of Nawangar (1872–1933) who learned cricket in India, attended Cambridge University, and played on the English national team against Australia. In 1907 "Ranji" came home to India to assume the duties of Maharaja and to promote cricket in India. By the 1930s cricket was the major urban sport of the subcontinent, and it is interesting that the Indians who later argued for national independence used sports terms like "fair play" and "not cricket" to persuade British authorities about the right for self rule.

## Soccer, the world's game

The diffusion of the world's most popular game, soccer, however, was much broader. After development in the English boy's schools soccer crossed the English Channel where it was taught in schools by transplanted English schoolmasters and by students who had been to England. In Belgium the game spread through the Roman Catholic school system and in the Netherlands through sports clubs. Students in Germany eagerly took up soccer to replace boring calisthenics and during the 1880s Britons and Germans established clubs for young adults. Englishmen in Paris formed a Paris Football Association Club in 1887 and inspired French schoolboys to form their own team the next year.

In Rotterdam port workers learned the game from British sailors while miners and steel workers in the Ruhr took up the game they learned from their children. In Italy British sailors played soccer in the port cities. English merchants organized the first clubs such as the famous Juventus Football Club of Turin, and Italian businessmen brought home balls from their trips to England. Charles Lowenrosen, a schoolboy whose parents immigrated to England from Hungary, returned to Budapest for a visit in 1896 with a soccer ball. Three months later his friends formed the first Hungarian team. Soccer thus captured the attention of all classes in Europe.

In 1903, Robert Guerin, a leader in French athletics, suggested to Frederick Wall, the secretary of the Football Association in England that an international organization should be formed. Although condescendingly rejected Guerin went forward in 1904 to put together with France, Belgium, Denmark, Holland, Spain, Sweden, and Switzerland the *Fédération Internationale de Football Association* (FIFA) that has become the largest and most significant of the world sports federations. It now includes over 200 member countries, about the same as the United Nations. Britain joined in 1906, left briefly in 1920 to protest German and Austrian membership, and huffed out again in 1928–1946 in opposition to broken-time payments.

Love for the game penetrated so deep that during the remarkable "Christmas truce" of 1914 in World War I soldiers from both sides along the western front came out of the wet trenches to play soccer with each other amid the shell holes of no man's land. It was a spontaneous ceasefire inspired by the goodwill of Christmastime that bubbled up from the lower ranks. Officers could not stop it and the cross-trench fraternization threatened their authority. What if the soldiers discovered the humanity of their enemy and refused to fight? It was halted with orders to fire the artillery from behind the lines to break up the games and by rotating the tainted troops away from the front.

## Soccer in Africa

Both the colonial French and British introduced soccer into Africa, mainly to elite male students in the cities. French Catholic missionaries introduced soccer to give young converts something to do after school. It was fun, cheap, easy to learn and became a part of street culture in Brazzaville in the Congo. There were 11 independent township teams by 1931 and the colonial authority set up the Native Sports Federation to provide French direction for the clubs. Frenchmen volunteered to coach, but during the Great Depression siphoned off funds to support the white teams. To maintain superiority and assert authority French officials banned the use of cleats by black players in 1936. For the blacks this was an insult and yet another example of an overbearing ruler. After World War II and decolonization, they got their shoes back. In the northern countries of Tunisia and Algeria soccer became a sport for the local rebels. They thought that if they could win at soccer, they could win at warfare. They used their clubs to plot revolution and obtained publicity through soccer to aid in their struggle to overturn French rule.

The British military commanders in Africa used sports, particularly soccer, for physical conditioning, self discipline, to let off steam, and to dampen the sex drive of the soldiers. This applied to the black recruits as well. Imperial administrators were often selected for their athleticism and teachers used sports for character training, maintaining discipline, and teaching good manners. Although not much is known about pre-colonial sports in Africa the indigenous pastimes included foot races, wrestling, canoe races, jumping, and dancing. The new Western sports supplanted these. Cecil Earle Tyndale-Biscoe, the headmaster of the Tanga School in Tanzania in 1925, for instance, introduced his boys to boxing in order to reduce bullying and sodomy, and used soccer as a part of everyday life for character training. The Union of South Africa began a Football Association in 1892, Kenya started one in 1922, and Egypt participated in the 1934 World Cup. Durban and Johannesburg sprouted workplace teams and a Bantu Football Association formed in 1929. During the next decade the association sponsored nearly 500 junior and senior teams.

At the time of decolonization in Africa Egypt, Ethiopia, South Africa, and the Sudan in 1957 formed the *Confédération Africaine de Football* that sponsored the African Nations Cup, a soccer tournament held every two years. Because of multi-racial prejudice South Africa withdrew until 1992, but other nations joined into the cup competition. Civil disorder and poverty in Africa have disrupted much of the effort to develop sports teams and the best players have migrated to Europe. FIFA, for instance, selected emigrant George Weah from Liberia who played for Milan as the World Player of the Year in 1995. Cameroon, Nigeria, Senegal, South Africa, Morocco, Tunisia, and Ivory Coast, nonetheless, were ranked by FIFA among the top 50 soccer nations in 2001 and Senegal made it to the quarter-finals in the 2002 World Cup competition.

## Soccer in India

The British who occupied India for much of the modern period with as many as 75,000 soldiers, played soccer and other sports for fitness and morale. Service in the subcontinent could be tedious and as one old trooper put it, "We had one great weapon against boredom. The answer was sport, sport, sport." Soccer clubs formed in Calcutta, the first in 1878, and elsewhere in the next few decades. The Indian Football Association began in 1893 and by 1929 it included 140 Indian and 14 European teams. In 1911, Mohan Bagan, a native Bengali team, defeated the East Yorkshire Regiment team before a crowd of 50,000. The Indians, of course, wildly celebrated this victory over their masters, and the British had the opportunity to show their famous restrained good sportsmanship. In contrast, in austere Tibet the British were unable to gain acceptance of either soccer or cricket. The Buddhist monks saw foreign influence and games as a threat to their culture and the Tibetan government actually banned soccer in 1944.

## Polo and India

While in India, British officers in Assam, incidentally, witnessed the native horseback game of "pulu" played by hitting a willow-root ball up and down a field with sticks. Games of this sort had been played centuries ago in Persia and China. The officers refined the game of "polo" by designating four horsemen per side, putting up goal posts, developing long-handled mallets, evolving rules of right-of-way to protect horses and riders, and dividing a match into six periods called "chukkas," a word of Indian origin. The game spread quickly among the maharajahs, English tea planters, and British soldiers. An Indian polo club started in the district of Cachar in 1859 and a British club began in Calcutta in 1862. It was considered good training for cavalry.

The Tenth Hussars and the Ninth Lancers gave a demonstration in England at Hounslow Heath in 1870—a match noted more for strong language than for strong play. James Gordon Bennett, Jr, an American bon vivant, observed a match and took the concept home, along with sample equipment and a coach, to his rich friends at Newport, Rhode Island in 1875. The result was the Westchester Cup, an international match between the United States and Great Britain that began in 1886 and has been contested sporadically since then. British ranchers took polo to Argentina in the 1870s where it became a part of the military tradition. Buenos Aires, subsequently, became the world center of polo in the twentieth century and the Argentine Open that began in 1893 became the most prestigious tournament in the world.

## Soccer in South America

Skilled young Britons traveled to Latin America as engineers and merchants and by the late nineteenth century there was a British community of 40,000 in Buenos Aires where soccer naturally became a part of the foreign English schools. Alexander Watson Hutton from Scotland became a part of this migration when he joined the faculty of St Andrew's College in Buenos Aires in 1881. In 1884 he opened an English high school that included in the curriculum tennis for girls and soccer for boys. He sent home for equipment and when the soccer balls arrived the puzzled customs officials labeled them "items for the crazy English." The game flourished and in 1893 Hutton organized a league that became the Argentine Football Association. The group later translated the name to Spanish, but remembered Hutton as "the father of Argentine soccer."

By 1907 there were 300 soccer clubs in Buenos Aires. With kids playing in the barrios and streets, a style of "criollo," or creole soccer evolved that was noted for its spontaneity and flair. It contrasted to the English form that used physical strength and dogged persistence on the field. The clubs became social and political centers associated with political parties, and the politicians who saw the fans as voters granted money for the building of club stadiums. Soccer success has been linked, consequently, with the success and failure of dictator Juan Domingo Peron (1895–1974).

In Montevideo, British engineers and managers set up schools that supported soccer and founded the Uruguayan Football Association in 1900. In Brazil, Charles Miller, born in Brazil and educated in England, brought home a soccer ball and persuaded the Sao Paulo Athletic Club to form a soccer section. Other small teams formed in the late 1890s and they came together in a league in 1901. The same process occurred at Rio de Janeiro where the European sons of local leaders set up athletic clubs that featured soccer, but also embraced cycling, billiards, regattas, and horseracing.

The most famous soccer clubs were the white, exclusive Fluminense (1902) and the black, poor Flamengo (1911) that developed a biting rivalry that continues to the present time. Soccer teams sprouted in other South American regions, but the centers of activity were Rio de Janeiro, Sao Paulo, Buenos Aires, and Montevideo. A tournament organized by the Argentine Football Association in 1910 between Argentina, Chile, and Uruguay led to the formation of *Confederacion Sudamericana de Futbol* that in 1916 hosted a South American championship at Buenos Aires. This regional effort along with transnational tournaments in Europe inspired the global competition of the World Cup, the most important sporting event outside of the Olympics.

## The World Cup and Pele

The Olympic Games excluded professional players, so Jules Rimet, the French president of FIFA proposed an open championship to be played every fourth year. FIFA agreed and selected Uruguay as the site. The South American country offered to pay travel and accommodation expenses, but only Belgium, France, Romania, and Yugoslavia arrived from Europe. In this first World Cup of 1930 there were 13 entries, and in the final competition between Uruguay and Argentina, Uruguay emerged as the winner. In 1994 there were 138 teams competing for a place in the World Cup playoffs. Of the total of 17 World Cup championships South American countries have won nine (Uruguay 2, Argentina 2, Brazil 5).

The reason for Brazil's dramatic success was due largely to the skill of the best soccer player in the history of the sport—Edson Arantes do Nascimento, otherwise known as "Pele." He was born in 1940 in northeastern Brazil, dropped out of school in the fourth grade, and went to work as an apprentice shoemaker. His father, however, loved soccer and taught his son the game. "Brown professionalism," the use of mulatto professional players, had been established in the 1920s and soccer became both a symbol for a successful, racially mixed society and a ladder of social mobility. Showing enormous talent for the game he called "the greatest joy of the people," Pele quickly began playing in 1956 with the major league Santos club. "Many times, people ask me where I come from," he commented. "This is a very hard question, because the answer is nothing. I come from nothing, because where I grew up in Brazil was a very poor place in the middle of nowhere. Also my nickname means nothing. Pele. It is just a word."

Brazil drafted him for the national team in 1958 and he carried them to a World Cup triumph while the fans in Sweden chanted, "Pele!, Pele!" He was instantly world famous and led the Brazilian team to other World Cup championships in 1962 and 1970. He scored a goal in almost every game of his career. To illustrate his extraordinary talent—in a league game in Brazil in 1959 he took a pass at midfield, kicked the ball repeatedly in the air, went through and around various defenders, faked the goaltender, and put the ball into the net for a score without once letting the ball touch the ground. Pele retired in 1974, but returned to the soccer field in 1975–1978 to play with the New York Cosmos in a failed attempt to establish professional soccer in the United States.

## Soccer and the United States

The lack of soccer success in the United States when it is so popular everywhere else has long been a sports question. The general answer is that soccer was crowded out by American football, basketball, and baseball—indigenous sports that prideful Americans preferred to foreign sports. By the time soccer was developed and exported to the United States the home sports were established. Some immigrants, however, continued to play soccer for their own amusement, and in the late 1970s it became an activity of upper-class high schools and colleges. Amateur soccer was cheap, safe, and healthy and it took root in middle-class suburbs as well—hence the birth of the so-called "soccer mom" who ferried her progeny to scattered fields in vans and station wagons. With the rise of concern for sports equality for women, moreover, soccer became a sport of choice for girls.

To boost this rising interest FIFA awarded the World Cup playoffs to the United States in 1994, and a professional men's league began again in 1996. The Women's United Soccer Association (WUSA), buoyed by an Olympic victory in 1996 and a World Cup championship in 1999, began play in 2001. Although FIFA recognized the American star Mia Hamm as its first Women's World Player of the Year in 2001, WUSA collapsed in the fall of 2003 during the World Cup playoffs in the United States. Consequently, in spite of widespread youth participation soccer still sputters in a quest for acceptance in North America.

## Muscular Christianity

It is a tribute to British persistence that cricket and soccer were eventually accepted in India, at least with the male, big-city, upper class. At most, athletics for girls was an afterthought, and moreover, some 80 percent of the Indian population remained in traditional rural villages. Hinduism, furthermore, prohibited the use of leather made from a cow, an animal considered sacred. Both cricket balls and soccer balls were covered with cowhide.

In the late nineteenth century Cecil E. Tyndale-Briscoe, an Anglican missionary teacher in Kashmir, had to allow his boys to catch the cricket ball with their sleeves pulled over their hands to avoid being defiled. By forcing students to play Tyndale-Briscoe sought to inculcate British values and once threatened his students with a riding crop, herded them to a field, and required them to play soccer. A boy struck in the face with the ball had to be rushed by his classmates to a nearby canal to be washed and purified. Another defiled player was not allowed to return to his family and had to go live with relatives. After the British exodus from India in 1947 following a dominating presence of some 250 years they left behind a residue of law, technology, language, and sport that has endured. Still, the main religion is Hinduism, and the cow remains sacred. If nothing else this paradox is a reflection of the accommodating, diverse nature of Hinduism, and the globalization of sport.

British teachers such as Tyndale-Briscoe fervently believed in the benefit of sports for students. In the English boarding schools for elite boys such as Eton, Rugby, and Harrow after 1850 sports became a part of the curriculum and all pupils were expected to participate. A *Punch* cartoon from 5 October 1889 characterized this movement. It featured a headmaster berating an abashed student named Fitzmilksoppe, "Of course you needn't work," the master said, "but play you must and shall!" In part, the sports regimen was a means of school control. There were few extracurricular activities, and unruly students were often a menace to the neighborhood. Harrow boys threw stones at passing ponies, cats, dogs, and workmen. At Marlborough on the first day of school the students beat all the local frogs to death and piled up the bodies in front of the school. Sports gave restless students something to do and at Harrow the boys actually asked for implementation of athletic activity.

But sports meant more than just school discipline. At Uppingham the headmaster, Edward Thring (1821–1887) believed in the education of the whole boy—"health of body, health of intellect, health of heart all uniting to form the true man." Thomas Arnold (1795–1842) the influential headmaster at Rugby wanted to produce Christian gentlemen who would be champions of righteousness. Sports participation was a part of this formative effort. Charles Kingsley (1819–1875), novelist, poet, and finally Canon of Westminster, summed it up:

> Through sport boys acquire virtues which no books can give them; not merely daring and endurance, but, better still, temper, self-restraint, fairness, honour, unenvious approbation of another's success, and all that 'give and take' of life which stand a man in good stead when he goes

forth into the world, and without which, indeed, his success is always maimed and partial.

Christian religiousness combined with sports became "muscular Christianity," a term Kingsley disliked, but which reflected school programs of practical recreation and Christian belief. With these embedded ideas the English schools produced the administrators, businessmen, teachers, and military officers who ran the British Empire and dispersed British culture to the world.

## The YMCA missionaries and China

It was at this time that the YMCA began its remarkable global spread. The organization, rooted in Britain, Canada, and the United States, was driven by a Christian missionary zeal that carried an imperative to teach basketball, volleyball, table tennis, and swimming. By 1890 there were some 400 YMCA gymnasiums in the United States and Canada—it was quite all right to entice young men with a gym to reach them with a Christian message. In 1900 there were associations on every continent including 16 in South America, 19 in Africa, 20 in Australia, and 270 in Asia. After enduring two world wars when the YMCA provided tons of recreational equipment to soldiers and prisoners of war in 1949 the "Y" had over 10,000 associations mainly in Europe and North America, but with 24 in South America, 61 in Africa and the Near East, 42 in Australia, and 502 in Asia. Starting in 1855, in addition, Christian women followed with a parallel organization, the Young Women's Christian Association and although it can now be found in 80 countries it does not seem to have had the same global impact for sports as the men's organization.

Outside workers, foreign businessmen, and YMCA deputies often started the associations for religious communion. The associations frequently supported, but did not join local Christian missions, and worked toward the construction of a building with "Y" amenities that upheld their four-fold program of addressing the spiritual, mental, social, and physical aspects of life. The establishment of YMCAs in world cities beyond the West sprinkled the globe: Calcutta (1854), Colombo (1859), Beirut (1861), Rio de Janeiro (1873), Bombay (1875), Osaka (1880), Seoul (1899), St Petersburg (1900), Buenos Aires (1901), Sao Paulo (1902), Mexico City (1902), Havana (1905), Manila (1907), and Cairo (1909). There were 2 associations in China in 1902, and 30 by 1920, 13 of which possessed buildings. Today, the YMCA can be found in 89 countries, but it did not conquer the world. There was resistance to Christian doctrine in Muslim countries and in 1950 the Communist Chinese eliminated the YMCA in China. Nonetheless, as an agency that propagated sports, particularly basketball and volleyball, as well as propagating the gospel the accomplishment of the YMCA was impressive.

In Asia the YMCA and the Christian missionaries who taught modern sports along with the ideas of sportsmanship and fair play had to overcome a cultural aversion for physical activity. There was a long intellectual antagonism toward physical exertion. Labor was for the lower classes. Large muscles and nakedness were not admired—it was not until 1986 that the Chinese government allowed women bodybuilders to wear bikinis in competition. Gentlemen and ladies wore long gowns and women were taught to walk deliberately with steps no more than a foot's length and with no swinging of the arms. The feet of upper-class girls were bound from birth to give them the tiny feet esteemed by men. The custom, of course, crippled the women. After a sweaty demonstration of tennis by diplomats in the late nineteenth century King Sunjong of Korea commented, "It is really pitiable for them to do such Herculean work for themselves. Those kind of things are assignable only to servants."

Among the lower classes, as might be suspected, there was a long heritage of physical recreation and training. Horsemanship and archery were necessary military skills. Wrestling, polo, ice skating in northern provinces, boxing, tugs of war (rope pulls), weight lifting, and *cuju*, a game similar to soccer, were used for soldier's conditioning. Among the people, *wushu*, or martial arts, flourished along with pastimes of fishing, boating, board games, and dancing. Festivals featured acrobatics, pole climbs, kite flying, dragon and lion dances, and dragon boat races. There was little inhibition against female participation, even for those with bound feet, and it is understandable that most of the current Chinese female athletes come from the lower classes that possessed an athletic tradition.

American and English Christian missionary schools introduced Western sports with their male bias in the 1880s, and in 1890 St Johns University of the Christian Church in Shanghai held a track meet. The YMCA provided trained physical education personnel and in 1896 introduced basketball in Tientsin, a treaty port for foreign commerce since 1860. Max J. Exner, a former roommate of James Naismith who took over the American Shanghai association in 1908 for three years, set up a two-year physical education training course for YMCA members, and established athletic facilities on the outskirts of the city. There were 14 students in his first class, and his facilities included a quarter-mile track, soccer field, four tennis courts, locker room, and gymnasium.

Exner organized a National Athletic Meet for China that featured tennis, soccer, basketball, and track and field for men in 1910. There were some 40,000 spectators. Europeans served as officials and when Sun Booxin, a high jumper, kept knocking the bar off with his queue, he was advised to cut it off. He did, and the next day he won. Exner wanted "to secure for the individual the basis for the largest and most efficient life for which it is possible for him to live, and to increase the capacity of the race."

The YMCA set up through its network the first Far Eastern Championships in Manila for China, Japan, and the Philippines in 1913. This predecessor to the post World War II Asian Games was the first international competition in the Far East and it featured track and field, swimming, tennis, baseball, basketball, volleyball, and soccer. There were 150,000 spectators and thus the games demonstrated sports competition for the masses of people. The YMCA organized a second National Athletic Meet in 1914, and another Far Eastern Championship for Shanghai in 1915. At the 1924 National Athletic Meet women participated in basketball, softball, volleyball, and group gymnastics. By and large Chinese officials ran the championships in 1924, and in 1927–1928 the government took control of physical education. YMCA influence declined after this point, but its efforts of 30 years had managed to introduce Western sports in Asia.

## Table tennis and the return of China

The history of China in the first half of the twentieth century is marked by the struggles between the Nationalists and the Communists, and the interruptions of civil war, World War II, and the Korean War. Chang Kai-Shek, the Nationalist Party leader, saw physical education and sports as a means to health, unity, and military strength. Mao Zedong, the Communist Party leader, related fitness to military strength and advocated 30 minutes of regular, simple exercise. International competition, however, practically ceased for about two decades after the Communist takeover in 1949 due to internal turmoil. The Chinese continued to compete sporadically in table tennis and invited some competition, such as a British swimming team in 1957. The situation changed dramatically, however, in 1971.

At the world table tennis championships in Japan a Chinese official quietly asked Jack Howard, captain of the American team, if the Americans might like to tour China "so that we can learn from each other and elevate our standards of play." This was a surprise because China had not welcomed outsiders for 20 years, and in addition, the American team was not very good compared to teams from Asia. The People's Republic of China (PRC) had just won four of six categories and the United States was far down the line. There was not much that they could learn from the Americans. Nevertheless, with the permission of the United States government 15 Americans, including 7 men and 2 women players toured China for 8 days.

They were treated with cordiality and met the Chinese premier, Zhou Enlai, who spoke to them about starting a new era of friendship with the United States. This shift in position coincided with a desire by China to join the United Nations, to reconnect with the world. The table tennis team returned home with the message, Secretary of State Henry Kissinger flew secretly to Beijing to make arrangements, and in 1972 President Richard M. Nixon made a formal visit. The "ping-pong diplomacy" was a success, and *Time Magazine* characterized the event as the "ping heard 'round the world."

## America's Cup and early transnational contests

Sports have often been a link between peoples. In 1851, for example, John Cox Stevens along with others constructed a $30,000 racing yacht called *America*. Stevens (1785–1857) a wealthy sports enthusiast who had set aside part of his family estate in Hoboken, New Jersey as a center for sports clubs, was the first "commodore" of the New York Yacht Club (NYYC). During the London Exposition of 1851 Stevens responded to the challenge of the Royal Yacht Club to a 58-mile race around the Isle of Wight in the English Channel. Although somewhat hesitant to face the fast *America* with its sharp bow and slanted masts the English yachtsmen provided a trophy, the Hundred Guinea Cup. After Stevens and his crew won the race Queen Victoria graciously visited the boat and congratulated the winners.

In 1857 the NYYC offered the trophy, renamed the America's Cup, as a prize for international yacht racing competition. The race was held irregularly with the NYYC invariably victorious until 1983 when using a technologically superior keel the *Australia II* won. Captain John Bertrand commented, "*Australia II* did not merely turn, or even turn fast. She whipped around . . . her winged keel magically almost on a dime." Following their triumph the Aussie sailors returned to the dock singing their popular anthem "Waltzing Matilda." The San Diego Yacht Club recovered the cup for the United States in 1987, but New Zealand won it in 1995. Interestingly enough, Switzerland, a land-locked country, took the cup in 2003. The America's Cup race is a rich man's competition. It costs at least $80 million for a reasonable effort, but the cup is one of the oldest and most prestigious prizes of international competition.

Periodic international competition occurred in other sports as well. The British Open for "the champion golfer of the world" began in 1860, the U.S. Open in 1895 and the Ryder Cup between the United States and Great Britain in 1927. The Wimbledon championships for tennis began in 1877 and the Davis Cup started in 1900.

## The modern Olympic Games

By far the most important modern development, however, was the reconstitution of the Olympic Games. It was the dream of Baron Pierre de Coubertin (1863–1937) a diminutive, 100 pound, aristocratic Frenchman who grew up in Paris at a time of French political reversals. Napoleon III failed to establish the Archduke Maximilian on a throne in Mexico, and in addition lost the Franco-Prussian War of 1870. The Germans besieged and bombarded Paris during this humiliation. In looking for a reason for the French losses Coubertin noted that German soldiers were in better physical condition than the French troops.

Earlier in 1810 Friedrich Ludwig Jahn (1778–1852) had built a *Turnplatz*, or playground, on the outskirts of Berlin to teach schoolboys to climb poles, ladders, and ropes in order to bolster their physical condition. It was the beginning of gymnastics and this form of physical education spread through the schools of central Europe. Jahn saw the exercises as a patriotic effort to overthrow the rule of the French conqueror, Napoleon I. Now ironically, nearly a century later, disciplined exercise was a French answer to German conquest.

The young baron believed the English myth that Napoleon's defeat at Waterloo resulted from lessons learned on the playing fields of Eton. In addition, in 1875–1881 German archaeologists uncovered much of the ancient Olympic site in Greece. They had found statues, ruins of buildings, and 1,300 gold objects that supported the stories about the Ancient Olympics and the fabled Olympic truce. These facts about sport mixed in Coubertin's mind and he began to think that a modern Olympic Games might be a key to world peace. He traveled widely in Europe, England, and the United States, spoke to sports leaders, wrote articles, and organized athletics in France.

At his urging some 78 delegates from 9 nations met at the Sorbonne in 1894. They argued about eligibility, agreed to form an International Olympic Committee (IOC), and awarded the first Olympiad to Greece for 1896. The self-regulating and self-selecting IOC was made up largely of older, rich, well-born, unpaid men who could financially support the effort. The Greeks had held a series of national games starting in 1859 funded by millionaire shipping magnate Evangelis Zappas. At his death in 1865 he left money to restore the ancient Greek stadium. This was the white marble, horseshoe-shaped stadium used for the first Olympics in 1896.

Although the exact numbers are open to question, about 70,000 spectators, and 311 athletes from 13 countries participated in the first modern Olympiad. Unlike the international championships for a particular sports the Olympics held a variety of events—track and field, fencing, cycling, gymnastics, shooting, swimming, tennis, weightlifting, and wrestling. There was a rope climbing event, and swimming took place in the 12-foot waves and chilling 55-degree water of the Bay of Zea. The Greeks won 47 medals and the United States finished in second place with 19.

The American team consisted of five men from the Boston Athletic Club, four from Princeton University, and James B. Connolly (1868–1957) who had to quit Harvard in order to compete. The school refused to give him time off for this obscure and unknown event. Connolly, nonetheless, joined with his teammates; had his wallet stolen in Naples; arrived the day before the meet started; stayed up all night; won the hop-skip-and-jump; and became the first Olympic champion in 1,500 years. When he returned home there was no one to meet him, but he possessed an Olympic medal and went on to a distinguished career as a writer and journalist. At the graduation ceremonies in 1949 Harvard University invited him to the platform, awarded him a Harvard athletic letter, and told him that they were sorry for the way they had treated him.

As in the ancient Olympics there were no events for women, but it did include a marathon race. A French historian suggested the long-distance run from the City of Marathon and 17 entrants started from the Marathon Bridge. A short, spindly mailman from Maroussi, Greece, Siridon Louys came in first with a time of 2 hours and 58 minutes. As he rounded into the stadium the local fans shouted, "Hellene! Hellene!" ("A Greek! A Greek!"). Crown Prince Constantine came out of the stands to accompany the runner to the finish and King George of Greece later gave him a horse and cart for mail delivery. Noting the enthusiasm of the Greeks for Louys, French writer Charles Maurras said to Coubertin as he watched the celebration, "I see that your internationalism . . . does not kill national spirit—it strengthens it." It was a prophecy.

Following the brief tenure of Dimitrios Vikelas, a Greek intellectual, Coubertin presided as president of the IOC from 1896 until 1925. In 1913 Coubertin designed the famous five-interlocked rings logo of the Olympics to represent the five segments of the world won to Olympism, and in 1921 a French cleric suggested the motto, *citius, altius, fortius* (swifter, higher, stronger). The ever-optimistic Coubertin endured the disillusionment of World War I and saw to the celebration of the Sixth Olympiad in Antwerp in 1920.

As a patriarch Coubertin resisted the participation of women in the games, but allowed women's demonstration events for tennis and golf in 1900, archery in 1904, tennis, archery and figure skating in 1908, and swimming and diving in 1912. Meanwhile, Alice Milliat of France organized several "Women's Olympic Games" between 1921 and 1934. Women athletes were thus grudgingly accepted albeit with fewer events. In 1932 there were six women's events in track and field; in 1948 there were only nine. In 2000, 42 percent of the athletes in the summer Olympics were women and they competed in 121 events.

Coubertin also opposed the designation of a permanent site for the games, inclusion of professional athletes, or a separate Winter Olympic Games although figure skating had been demonstrated in 1908 and 1920. A modest winter sports festival (later designated the first Winter Olympics), nonetheless, took place in 1924 in Chamonix, France and winter athletics became an official part of the Olympics in 1928. For 30 years Coubertin had directed the fate of the games, but it was now going beyond him. He resigned the presidency in 1925, lived on as an honored founder of the movement, and directed at his death that his heart be removed from his body and entombed at Olympia, the site of the ancient games in Greece.

The Olympic Games have continued to the present time. In 2002, 78 nations participated in the Winter Olympics; in 1924 there were 16. At the summer Olympics in 2000 there were 199 nations; in 1896 there were 13. The number of events has increased well over tenfold. Host nations have been allowed to introduce demonstration sports and the IOC has added others. For example, baseball began in 1992, basketball in 1936, and women's soccer in 1996. Judo was introduced at the Tokyo Olympics in 1964 and illustrated how a non-Western sport could become global.

## Judo and the Olympics

Although all peoples have developed some form of unarmed combat the Far East has been famous for martial arts that reached back into the seventh century. During the period of Japanese modernization at the end of the nineteenth century when foreign teachers introduced Western sports such as baseball, Kano Jigoro (1860–1938) synthesized and analyzed the common jujutsu techniques to create judo, a form of self defense that used an opponent's force against him. In 1882 Kano founded a school to teach his "way of gentleness" that was soon copied and became a middle-school physical education requirement.

He traveled widely to promote judo, founded the Japanese Amateur Athletic Association in 1911, and led Japan into the Olympic movement in 1909–1910. World War II scuttled the Olympic Games scheduled for Tokyo in 1940 and afterwards Americans temporarily suppressed judo during the occupation of the country. The sport revived, however, and 17 countries established the International Judo Federation in 1952. On its path to being accepted as a modern world sport judo modified its original purpose of maiming an opponent to allow contestants to survive without injury. In Dunning's terms judo became "civilized." A world championship was held in Japan in 1956 and judo became an Olympic sport eight years later. To the surprise of the Japanese, Anton Geesing, a Dutchman, won gold in the open category. The USSR, US, West Germany, South Korea, and Austria also won medals which attested to the global interest in the Asian martial art.

## Hitler and the Olympics

The periodic sequence of the games has been interrupted by warfare— the ultimate failure of diplomacy—and other major political events also have had influence on Olympic history. The IOC, generally, has attempted to avoid controversy, but political problems have been thrust upon it. At the 1936 Berlin Games, for example, dictator Adolf Hitler (1889–1945) used the Olympiad to publicize himself, the Nazi Party, and his concept of a superior Aryan race. The Nazis forced Jews out of the German sports clubs and treated blacks as inferior. When confronted about this prejudice by the IOC president, Henri de Baillet-Latour of Belgium, Hitler retorted, "When you are invited to a friend's home, you don't tell him how to run it, do you?" The IOC leader replied, "Excuse me, Mr. Chancellor, when the five rings are raised over the stadium, it is no longer Germany. It is the Olympics and we are masters there."

Hitler complied and assured the IOC and the president of the American Olympic Committee, Avery Brundage (1887–1975) that there would be no difficulty. Brundage had to stop a boycott of the games at home led by American Jews, Roman Catholics, and blacks. Usually the AAU selected and certified the Olympic team, but Brundage worried that a protest by the AAU would undercut the process had the Olympic Committee certify the American team. The United States sent athletes to both the winter and summer games in Germany and as it turned out there was no great difficulty. Baron de Coubertin sent a recorded message for the opening, "The important thing at the Olympic Games is not to win, but to take part, just as the important thing about life is not to conquer, but to struggle well." Norway won the most medals, 15, in the Winter Games; Germany won the most medals, 89, in the Summer Games.

To the delight of the United States, however, black American athletes disputed the concept of Aryan supremacy with sparkling performances. The outstanding competitor of the games was African-American James C. "Jesse" Owens (1918–1980). He ran with the grace of a gazelle and in one afternoon at Ohio State University he set three world records and tied a fourth. At the Berlin Olympics Owens won four gold medals—in the 100 and 200-meter sprints, long jump, and 400-meter relay. During the long jump competition he made friends with Luz Long, a German who came in second. To the discomfort of the Nazi spectators the blond Long walked arm-in-arm around the stadium with Owens.

At first Hitler made a show of congratulating the German winners, but the IOC asked him to stop and he did. Shortly before the awards ceremony for Cornelius Johnson and David Albritton, African-Americans who placed first and second in the high jump, Hitler and his entourage left the stadium supposedly because it was about to rain. Reporters interpreted this exit,

Owen's victories, and Hitler's halt in his public felicitations as a "snub" to Owens and other blacks. The journalists thus created one of the long-enduring myths about the 1936 Olympics. It makes little difference, however, since Hitler proclaimed in one of his propaganda sheets, "The Americans ought to be ashamed of themselves for letting their medals be won by Negroes. I myself would never shake hands with one of them." Later, Owens who returned to a segregated United States commented laconically, "I wasn't invited to shake hands with Hitler, but I wasn't invited to the White House to shake hands with the President, either."

## Racism and the Olympics

The Olympics reflected world race problems on other occasions. Racism in sports is quite visible and people have used the Olympic spotlight to point up their causes. At the 1968 Mexico City Games African-American sprinters Tommie Smith and John Carlos mounted the victor's stand after placing first and third in the 200 meters, bowed their heads, and raised a fist covered with a black glove to protest racial conflict within the United States. This was the echo of a failed attempt to organize a boycott of Olympic participation by African-American athletes. Ironically, the Mexico City Olympiad is noted as the time when African runners came to dominance. African men won every distance event over 800 meters. More significant, however, was the IOC ban of the Union of South Africa for its apartheid policies of black-white segregation.

Racial taboos in sport broke down everywhere in the world in the 1950s, but not in South Africa. In 1963 white and black sports people in South Africa formed the upstart South African Non-Racial Olympic Committee (SANROC) and asked the IOC to expel the sanctioned, white South African National Olympic Committee. Avery Brundage, now the president of the IOC (1952–1972), personally thought that racial discrimination was insufficient for expulsion and that the "games must go on" regardless of conditions.

The IOC under pressure from newly formed black African nations, however, insisted that there should be no discrimination—equality was a long-standing Olympic ideal—and withdrew the invitation for South Africa to participate in the 1964 Tokyo Games. A threatened boycott by African nations and the communist bloc in 1968 resulted in banning South Africa from the Mexico City Olympiad. World resistance continued to mount against South Africa and touring rugby teams sent to England (1969–1970), Australia (1971), and New Zealand (1981) had to run the gauntlet of protestors. In 1970 the IOC expelled South Africa with a 35:28 vote. In 1976, 28 African teams returned home just before the opening of the Montreal Olympics to protest the inclusion of New Zealand that had played rugby games with South Africa, even though rugby was not an Olympic sport.

In 1990, F. W. de Klerk (1936–), president and leader of the conservative white National party in South Africa, began negotiations with the banned black African National Congress to end the segregation of the country and in 1991 the IOC restored South Africa to membership. In 1994 South Africa held a democratic election and Nelson Mandela, the new black president, in 1995 wore a green and gold Springbok jersey, a symbol of earlier white sports, to view the world rugby championship when South Africa beat New Zealand. Desmond Tutu, the great black South African Anglican archbishop, commented, "I did not expect this, but I am proud to wear [a Springbok jersey] when a few years ago, even a few months ago, it was anathema . . . No one of us could ever in their wildest dreams have been able to predict that rugby . . . could have this magical effect."

## Violence and the Olympics

There were additional conflicts between countries that often used the Olympics as a stage. Mainland China wished to exclude Taiwan and a two-China policy had to be worked out in 1978–1981; East Germans and West Germans competed as a joint team in 1960 and 1964 despite the division of the Berlin Wall (1962); North Koreans and South Koreans refused to cooperate.

In addition, on 2 November 1956 the USSR sent tanks into Hungary to suppress rebellion against Soviet leadership followed by mass arrests and deportations. Some 200,000 Hungarians fled to the West. Meanwhile, in December, Hungary faced the USSR in water polo at the Melbourne Olympics. Hungarian expatriates crowded the natatorium and the game deteriorated with foul play from the beginning. Fighting broke out all over the pool during the second half and in the final moments a USSR swimmer slugged Ervin Zador with his fist and split open the Hungarian's forehead. Blood stained the water red. Officials called in the police to handle the screaming spectators, and later 45 members of the 175-person Hungarian delegation sought asylum. Miklos Martin, one of the defectors, commented about the USSR, "They play their sports just as they conduct their lives—with brutality and disregard for fair play."

The worst bloodshed, however, occurred during the 1972 Munich Games. Palestinian terrorists entered the Olympic village, killed two Israeli coaches, and took hostage seven Israeli athletes and two security officers. For 23 hours the terrorists bargained for the release of 234 Palestinian prisoners and then fled with the hostages to Fürstenfeldbruck airport. There, in a shootout with German sharpshooters, all the hostages died along with five of the eight terrorists. One of the terrorists blew up the helicopter containing the hostages with a grenade. Brundage in his last public act as head of the IOC declared that the Olympics must never bow to criminal pressure and that "the Games must go on." There was a memorial service in the stadium; the competition continued; and American swimming officials surrounded Mark Spitz, an American Jew who won seven gold medals and set seven Olympic records in the pool, and flew him to England for safety.

## The Cold War and the Olympics

The Olympic strife in the second half of the twentieth century took place in the overall context of the Cold War between the United States and the Soviet Union. Both nations tried to prove their superiority by constructing complex war machinery, training large armies, and providing money, treaties, and technology for supposed allies. Sports competition became enmeshed in the larger competition of the Cold War. After all, on the world stage the greatest nation would naturally produce the greatest athletes, or so the logic implied. It was a way to express the vitality of the nation.

The Soviets sent observers to the 1948 London Games and then appeared with a full team at Helsinki in 1952. There, the United States won 76 medals and the USSR took 69. After this, with the exception of the Mexico Games in 1968, the Soviets beat the United States in head-to-head Olympic competition in the winter games as well as in the summer games through 1992. At the 1992 Barcelona Games 12 of the former Soviet republics of the collapsed USSR formed a temporary united team that captured the leading number of medals.

The Soviet Union was able to excel in Olympic athletics by focusing a national effort to create champions. For Joseph Stalin (1879–1953), the communist dictator, success in international sports was a matter of successful foreign policy. This did not change after his death. Coaches would be purged and teams disbanded for losing, but the USSR was never as sports obsessed as it seemed to the outside world. According to historian Robert Edelman in his study of sports in the USSR, *Serious Fun* (1993), success in the Olympics brought prestige to the country, but Soviet fans were interested mainly in soccer, basketball, and ice hockey. Women's sports attracted little following.

British seamen in the Baltic Sea had introduced soccer in the 1860s and the opening of the summer soccer season became a welcome celebration for Russians. Soldiers even played matches on 2 May 1942 before 8,000 fans during the siege of Leningrad with German armies hammering at the gate. The YMCA taught basketball in Latvia, Estonia, and Lithuania after World War I and the USSR annexed those countries in 1939. Soviet schools took up the game and the Soviets dominated European amateur basketball from the 1950s into the 1970s.

Ice hockey became popular in Europe in the 1930s after the successful Winter Olympics at St Moritz in 1928. The Soviet skaters with no artificial ice rink until 1956 developed a style of synchronous "skate and pass" that contrasted to the Canadian style of "bump and fight" that brought the USSR to world prominence. In 1972 the USSR and Canadian all-star professionals played an eight-game home-and-home series in which Canada won four, lost three, and tied one. This meant that the Soviet ice hockey skaters were as good as the best in the world, but no better.

The Olympic sports, thus, were a facade as far as the Soviet citizen was concerned. The government, nonetheless, ordered spectacular sports festivals, such as the *Spartakiad* and sent young athletes to sports boarding schools or clubs where they could be nurtured by improved facilities and instruction. If useful, birth dates were falsified. The goal to win medals justified any method necessary. Sport was organized for efficiency and achievement, a reflection of the detailed planning found elsewhere in Soviet society.

Dinamo in Moscow became a notorious sports club sponsored by the security forces where the athletes were full-time employees, offered bonuses for winning, given performance-enhancing drugs, and told that they were amateurs. The TsSKA (Central Sports Club of the Army) performed the same sports development for the Soviet armed forces and became particularly noted for its ice hockey teams that won every Olympic championship between 1956 and 1992 with the exception of US victories in 1960 and 1980. The East Germans, and later the Chinese copied the Soviet sports model. At the 1976 Montreal Games, East Germany, with a population of less than 17 million gathered more medals than the United States. The communists, therefore, focused upon the task of winning by any possible means and cynically exploited the amateur ideal of the Olympics.

The weird boycotts of the 1980 and 1984 Games resulted directly from Cold War politics and achieved little other than frustration for the athletes. The USSR had been awarded the Olympic Games for 1980, spent millions of rubles in preparation, and anticipated the opportunity to demonstrate the triumph of communism to the world. Late in 1979, however, the Soviets sent military forces into neighboring Afghanistan to buttress a communist government under threat by Islamic rebels. United States President Jimmy Carter called for a world boycott of the Moscow Games and 62 nations responded. The IOC refused to become embroiled in the politics, but the USOC reluctantly acceded to the boycott. Seventy-three percent of the American athletes patriotically agreed with some grumbling. It was the athletes who were hurt and hurdler Edwin Moses lamented, "These are *our* games." An athlete has a limited number of years to be at the top and for many this chance was now lost.

China, Israel, Canada, West Germany, and the Islamic nations lined up behind Carter. Great Britain's parliament agreed with the American President, but the independent Olympic committee sent a team anyway. Italy, France, Australia, and most of the African nations traveled to Moscow. The games were greatly diminished and there were rumblings about biased Soviet judges. Still, there were some high points such as when Great Britain's Steve Ovett beat his archrival Sebastian Coe in the 800-meter run and lost to Coe in the 1,500-meter race.

In a tit-for-tat the USSR led a 17-nation Eastern bloc boycott of the 1984 Los Angeles Games. Again the games were lessened without full global participation, but there were high moments such as Joan Benoit's victory in the first women's marathon and Mary Lou Retton's smiling triumph in gymnastics. These women became American superstars and energized the effort to promote women's athletics within the country.

When the Cold War ended in 1989–1991 with the collapse of the Soviet Union the great sports machines of the USSR and East Germany fell apart. Sports competition continued in the summer Olympiads at Seoul, Barcelona, Atlanta, and Sydney as well as the winter Games at Calgary, Albertville, Lillehammer, Nagano, and Salt Lake City. Recently there have been about 10,000 athletes participating in the summer games and about 2,000 athletes in the winter games. Over one-third of the participants are women. The success of the Olympics, moreover, spawned lasting regional interim sports festivals such as the Asian Games (1951–), Pan American Games (1951–), Maccabiah Games (1932–), and the Commonwealth Games (1930–).

There have been incidents of controversy after 1992, but without the grim shadow of the nuclear holocaust threatened by the Cold War. The Olympic Games, albeit buffeted by the politics, had passed through that era intact, but they were not the same. Much had changed not only about the Games, but also about sports.

## Further reading

William J. Baker, "To Pray or to Play? The YMCA Question in the United Kingdom and the United States, 1850–1900," *International Journal of the History of Sport*, vol. 11 (April 1994), pp. 42–62; William J. Baker and James A. Mangan, eds., *Sport in Africa* (New York: Africana, 1987); Douglas Booth, *The Race Game: Sports and Politics in South Africa* (London: Cass, 1998); Robert Edelman, *Serious Fun: A History of Spectator Sports in the USSR* (New York: Oxford, 1993); Allen Guttmann, *Games and Empires* (New York: Columbia, 1994); Allen Guttmann, *The Olympics: A History of the Modern Games* (Urbana: University of Illinois, 2002); Allen Guttmann and Lee Thompson, *Japanese Sports* (Honolulu: Hawaii, 2001); Victor Heiser, *An*

*American Doctor's Odyssey* (New York: Norton 1936); Elmer L. Johnson, *The History of YMCA Physical Education* (Chicago: Association Press, 1979); Jonathon Kolatch, *Sports, Politics, and Ideology in China* (New York: Jonathan David, 1972); Richard S. Mandell, *The Nazi Olympics* (Urbana: University of Illinois, 1987); James A. Mangan, *Athleticism in the Victorian and Edwardian Public School* (Cambridge: Cambridge, 1981); James A. Mangan and Lamartine P. DaCosta (eds), *Sport in Latin American Society* (London: Cass, 2002); James Riordan (ed.), *Sport Under Communism* (London: Hurst, 1978); James Riordan and Robin Jones (eds), *Sport and Physical Education in China* (London: ISCPES, 1999); Stanley Weintraub, *Silent Night* (New York: Free Press, 2001).

# Chapter 5

# The Significance of Global Sports

World competition for the prestige of the state or for individual glory inspired changes for good and ill. Amateurism, the status of women, racial attitudes, technology, sports medicine, drug usage, the commercialism of sport, and sports architecture experienced major shifts, and it is with these changes that the importance of modern sports is found.

## Amateurism

The concept of amateurism evaporated in the heated friction of the Cold War. Earlier, the amateur ideal had caused difficulties with broken-time payments in English rugby and with poor American athletes. The most notorious episode in US history involved James F. "Jim" Thorpe (1888–1953), an American Indian of mixed Irish, French, and Sac-Fox tribal ancestry. He attended the Carlisle Indian School in Pennsylvania where he proved to be an outstanding all-around athlete. On the American Olympic team he won both the pentathlon and decathlon at the 1912 Stockholm Games. When King Gustav of Sweden presented him with his medals he said, "You sir, are the greatest athlete in the world." To the delight of anti-aristocratic Americans Thorpe replied simply, "Thanks, King."

To his misfortune the next year a reporter uncovered that Thorpe had played semiprofessional baseball during the summers for $15 per week. Although it was a common practice among college athletes of the time the acceptance of pay for sport meant that Thorpe was a professional. The Olympic officials who idolized amateurism demanded the return of his medals. Disgraced, Thorpe complied and went on to a career in professional football and baseball. Years later, after his death the IOC changed its position on amateurism and presented replica medals to his daughter.

It was the success of the Soviet sports machine that forced a different stance on amateurism in the West. When the USSR joined the Olympic movement in 1948 the IOC refused to oppose the professionalism of Soviet athletes. It was considered more important to have the USSR within the

Olympic family than outside of it. The United States, Great Britain, France and other Western states, still upheld an amateur ideal and, consequently, began to experience embarrassing losses to the Soviets. Within the US, moreover, a nasty three-cornered fight over the control of athletes developed between the United States Olympic Committee (USOC), the Amateur Athletic Union (AAU), and the National Collegiate Athletic Association (NCAA). The AAU and the NCAA jealously controlled their athletes, often the same individual, and refused to cooperate to the harm of the nation's international teams. After attempts at mediation failed Congress passed the Amateur Sports Act of 1978 to end the embroilment.

The act placed the USOC in overall control of Olympic sports and each sport was given its own national governing body. The governing bodies determined eligibility, sponsored meets, held workshops for coaches, and designated the Olympians for their sport. They were allowed to set up trust funds for individuals based upon prizes at meets and other earnings connected with the sport. The athlete could then draw upon the fund to pay training expenses. Although there were some differences between governing bodies concerning eligibility, the act essentially ended amateurism and allowed professionals to compete in the Olympics. Hence, the US sent professional women tennis players to the 1988 Seoul Games and a "Dream Team" of professional basketball stars to the 1992 Barcelona Games.

Amateurism withered elsewhere in the world, and in 1988 the USSR gave up the pretense as well. In that year, South Korea, Hungary, France, China, Spain, Poland, Malaysia, India, East Germany, and the Philippines began to give cash awards to their winners, and in 1993 the USOC offered to pay $15,000 to its gold medal Olympians. Today, the remnants of the amateur ideal are found mainly in the tortured restrictions for college and high school student-athletes.

## Race and ethnicity

Sports offered opportunity for ethnic athletes to boost national pride and to give their home country something to think about. Australia, for example, experienced the world-class talent of aboriginal athletes Evonne Goolagong in tennis and Cathy Freeman in track. Tennis coach Vic Edwards recognized the talent of Goolagong, daughter of a sheep-shearer, when she was nine years old. She moved in with Edwards' family when she was 14, and at age 19 she won singles at Wimbledon in 1971. The treatment of aborigines has been an embarrassing problem in Australian history and world-class sprinter Freeman carried an aboriginal flag during a victory lap at the 1994 Commonwealth Games. It was a defiant gesture to match the black power salute of Tommie Smith and John Carlos at the 1968 Mexico Olympics. "Being Aboriginal means everything to me," she said. "I feel for my people all the time. A lot of my friends have the talent, but lack the opportunity." Australian officials chose her to carry the torch into the stadium for the 2000 Sydney Olympics and to light the Olympic cauldron. For Freeman and Goolagong international athletics provided a ladder with which to climb from poverty and prejudice.

With the fall of the colonial empires after World War II African nations began to participate in international sports—21 in table tennis, 12 in soccer, 11 in track and field, 9 in swimming, 8 in basketball, and 8 in tennis. Participation in the Olympics became a measure of political maturity and the emerging African nations supported athletes by employment in police departments or military units, a system inherited from colonialism. They were aided by Western coaches and inspired by the coaching of Mal Whitfield, a US middle-distance runner sent to Africa as a cultural ambassador in the early 1960s. Historians Raymond Krise and Bill Squires state, "Mal Whitfield deserves honor not only as a two-time gold medallist at the Olympics and a peerless board runner, but also as the man who awoke an entire continent."

The first African to win an Olympic gold medal, Abebe Bikila (1932–1973) who was a body guard for Emperor Haile Selassie of Ethiopia, ran the marathon, over the cobblestones of the Appian Way bare-footed at the 1960 Rome Games in record time. Wearing shoes and socks he won again in 1964. At the 1968 Mexico City Games the Kenyan runners began their dominance of distance events with the victory of Kip Keino over Jim Ryun of the US in the 1,500-meter race. Ryun was the world record holder and had beaten Keino the year before. During the Olympic year, however, Ryun's training had been dampened by a case of mononucleosis. In Mexico City, Keino, who suffered from gallstones and an infection, was ordered by his doctor not to race, but at the last moment Keino changed his mind and took a taxicab to the stadium from the Olympic village. There was traffic congestion, the cab stalled, Keino got out and jogged to the starting line shortly before the race. The 7,300-foot altitude suited him—it was like that of his home in Kenya—and he was able to beat Ryun by three seconds to set an Olympic record. His victory inspired other Kenyan runners and began international experimentation with high-altitude training.

The Olympics, of course, had been open from the beginning to various races and ethnic groups. The Japanese, for example, sent two runners to the 1912 Stockholm Games, but they met with discouraging results. Kanaguri Shizo actually passed out when he paused to rest in the marathon and failed to finish the race. He felt humiliated and agonized about it for decades before he found a way to banish his shame. As reported by historians Allen Guttmann and Lee Thompson Kanaguri later returned to Stockholm, found the exact spot where he had quit and finished the race with a time of 55 years, 8 months, 6 days, and 32 minutes.

Kanaguri had actually continued to race in his younger years and completed the marathon to sixteenth place at the 1920 Antwerp Olympics. The team won a bronze medal in wrestling in 1924 and in 1928 won two golds, two silvers, and a bronze. The Japanese took a 131-person team to the 1932 Los Angeles Games and stunned the world by winning 11 of 16 possible medals in swimming. They had established a special elite training camp for swimmers and the Japanese had proven their capability. They won 18 medals at the Nazi Olympics in 1936, but their accomplishment had a poignant twist.

In Berlin, Korea's Sohn Kee-Chung, paced by the Englishman Ernest Harper, won the marathon in record time. Sohn had grown up as an oddity, running for pleasure along the banks of the Yalu River with rubber soles tied on his feet. This was odd because Korean custom called for slow, dignified walking, not running. Japan had taken over Korea in 1905 and to his distress Sohn had to run under the colors of Japan and with a Japanese name "Kitei Son." On the victory stand as the band played the Japanese anthem and raised the Rising Sun flag, Sohn, the first Korean champion, hung his head and wept for his lost country.

Such victories in the Olympics fed the fascination about race and athletics, a subject that continues to the present time. The great Jesse Owens was probed, measured, and x-rayed by a Cleveland doctor who concluded that Owen's physical advantages came from hard training, not racial inheritance. After the Berlin Olympics a physiological profile, however, determined that he should be a Norwegian. Racial matters in sports have proven to be enormously sensitive—enough to get sportscasters fired for offhand comments in the United States. Jimmy "the Greek" Snyder (1920–1996) said in a casual 1988 videotaped interview about the reason for superior black athletes, "During the slave period, the slave owner would breed his big black with his big woman so that he could have a big black kid—that's where it all started." The local television station broadcast his remarks on Martin Luther King, Jr Day in a program about African-American progress in America. Snyder inadvertently had stirred a hornets' nest of protest and CBS Sports fired him shortly after.

Still the debate continued, especially when fans observed that the number and success of black athletes in sports was disproportionate to their population numbers. The black population of the United States, for example, is 13 percent; the proportion of black players in Major League Baseball is 17 percent; the number in the National Basketball Association (NBA) is 80 percent; the distribution in the National Football League is 67 percent; and the share of black 1996 male track and field gold medallists is 93 percent.

Is the locker room cliché "White men can't jump, and black men can't swim", true? *Sports Illustrated*, the leading US sports magazine (1 July 1968,

5 August 1991 and 8 December 1997) had the courage to probe the question about the supposed superiority of black athletes, as did Tom Brokaw and NBC News with a documentary, "Black Athletes: Fact and Fiction," in April 1989. Friends warned Brokaw not to do the program and he later said, "There were times right before and after it aired that I worried if the storm would ever die down." It eventually did, but the debate continued unsettled.

The question of race in sports has been essentially a case of nature versus nurture. Are there significant genetic differences, or is it a circumstance of opportunity, coaching, and encouragement? There are always questions about proper research—for example, where do you find pure genetic samples, and how do you explain differences within the same group? The black Kenyans are superb distance runners and are physically much different from the black West Africans who seem to be the best sprinters. What about Hakeem Olajuwon, a superior professional basketball player from Nigeria in Central West Africa? And then, there is the case of Tiger Woods who is on his way to becoming a golfing legend. Earl, his father, is 50 percent African American, 25 percent American Indian, and 25 percent Chinese. Kutilda, his mother, is 50 percent Thai, 25 percent Chinese, and 25 percent white. Woods humorously refers to himself as a "Cablinasian." There are, consequently, no easy explanations about race and sports. There will always be exceptions, but the unsettling debate will likely continue into the future with some fire.

With a decline in prejudice and a greater acceptance of racial and ethnic differences, however, there has been a transnational flow of professional talent such as the seven-foot-five-inch basketball player Yao Ming from the Shanghai Sharks to the Houston Rockets in 2002. In the 2003 NBA draft 20 of the 58 first and second round choices came from outside the United States. In 1999 the Chelsea Club of London provided another example. The Italian manager fielded a multi-racial soccer team without a single British player in the lineup. Although sports may not have eliminated racial and ethnic prejudice, the success of these international stars has engendered respect and muted the tone of disapproval, at least for the members of the home team. Globalization has provided an economic opportunity for these elite male athletes and a lesson in diversity for humanity.

## Women and sports

The status of women has also changed. Generally, the nations with the greatest economic and social resources have more women athletes. Developing countries such as those in Africa, the sub-continent of India, and China, to a certain extent, where the women do much of the agricultural fieldwork and marry early have fewer athletes. Women have also been burdened with cultural restrictions in some places, such as in Islamic countries that keep them covered and secluded. In the last half of the twentieth century, under pressure of the Cold War, irreversible changes occurred.

At the 1976 Montreal Olympics where the United States came in third in the medal count, 35 percent of the USSR team and 40 percent of the East German team were women, while only 26 percent of the US team and 21 percent of the British team were women. The high death rate of Soviet men during World War II meant that women were readily taken for military service and physical work. There was therefore a ready acceptance of women in sport, and for international competition women's events presented an area to exploit.

The women of the USSR and East Germany won more than half of their team medals, and in the 17 track meet "duels" between the USSR and US (1958–1981) the Soviets depended upon their women to bring them victory. In contrast, in the United States there was a long-standing prejudice against women athletes. Diver Aileen Riggin recalled from 1920:

> It was not considered healthy for girls to overexert themselves or to swim as far as a mile. People thought it was a great mistake, that we were ruining our health, that we would never have children, and that we would be sorry for it later on.

This attitude about women continued until the US State Department recognized the reason for the Soviet athletic success and urged the USOC to do something to encourage American women to try sports. In 1960 Doris Duke Cromwell who inherited the Duke tobacco fortune gave $500,000 to the ill-funded USOC to investigate the problem. The concern of the state department coincided with a rising feminist movement and resulted in Title IX of the Educational Amendments Act of 1972. It simply stated: "No person in the United States shall, on the basis of sex, be excluded from participation in, be denied the benefits of, or be subjected to discrimination under any educational program or activity receiving federal financial assistance."

For sports it meant essentially that women should receive equal money and attention in athletic programs. It went into effect in 1975, attitudes began to shift, and the number of female athletes increased dramatically. By the end of the century the number of girls in high school sports had increased ten times, and the number of women in college athletics had increased five times. By 1988 women made up 40 percent of the US Olympic squad and began to match the communists stride for stride.

Inside the country, Title IX, as it became known, brought stress to athletic budgets since most colleges and many school districts received federal monies. Most schools made an effort to conform to the law, but there was no female sport that cost nearly as much as football, a male sport. Instead of expanding athletic budgets schools reduced men's sports in order to provide money for the women. Administrators eliminated men's gymnastics, wrestling, and swimming in particular, and preserved football under the assumption that this revenue generating activity supported the rest of the athletic program. In reality, only 13 percent of the NCAA's 524 football programs in 1989 covered their expenses. An NCAA study in 1997 revealed that less than half of the Division I-A and Division I-AA football programs paid for themselves. In 1999 journalists reported that only 41 percent of all football teams in Division I broke even, and that most athletic departments (94 percent) could not make it without supplemental student fees or general fund support.

Yet, Title IX and the women who wanted to be athletes were often blamed for the cuts in men's sports. In 1997 when Boston University ended its football program that was losing almost $3 million per year the administrators mentioned the loss of money, but blamed Title IX. Assistant Athletic Director Averill Haines who was in charge of women's athletics, however, countered, "There is not a female athlete that is not sharing in the disappointment and frustration we all feel. Nobody is dancing on graves." For Haines the reason for the women's sympathy for the abandoned Boston University football players was obvious—who could relate better to the lack of athletic opportunity than a woman?

There were various efforts to overturn Title IX—Tower Amendment, 1974; Javits Amendment, 1974; O'Hara Bill, 1975; Tower, Bartlett and Hruska Bill, 1977; Helms Bills, 1975, 1977. After the Supreme Court reduced coverage in Grove City vs Bell (1984), the Congress passed the Civil Rights Restoration Act in 1988 over the veto of President Ronald Reagan to reinforce the broad intention of Title IX to institutions of higher learning. In the Brown University Case of 1997 the Supreme Court rejected the argument that women really do not care to be athletes and dictated a rough parity between the number of females in a student body and the number of female athletes. Despite challenges, including a 2003 protest by wrestlers that culminated in an ad hoc presidential committee investigation, Title IX has been upheld. As such, this law that so affects half of the country's population can be counted as one of the most important enactments of the United States in the second half of the twentieth century.

What happened in the United States has been an important example for women in sports around the world, and is a part of the increasing global liberation of women. At the 2003 world track and field championships in Paris, for instance, Lima Azimi of Afghanistan competed in the first round of the 100-meter sprints. She wore a gray T-shirt, baggy pants, and her first pair of spiked shoes. She did not know how to use the starting blocks and at home she had been allowed to train only once a week in a gymnasium away from the presence of men. Still, she beat several other girls in a trial and Afghani officials asked her to go to Paris to represent the new country recently freed from Taliban control. Azima came in the slowest in eight heats by almost four seconds, but she was the first Afghan woman to participate in a major international sport. "The time didn't matter," she commented, "my participation was more important."

With the stunning success of the Kenyan male runners in the last part of the twentieth century the question arose, what about the Kenyan women? It was logical that there should be an equal number of great female runners, but there were none. The girls ran well in school, but a culture of early marriage and domesticity along with poverty sank their talents into quiet obscurity. A few began to break through and in 1991 Susan Sirma and Delillah Asiago won enough money in international road races in six weeks to make them millionaires at home. There has been a recent social shift and Pasqualine Wangui, a national marathon champion observed, "Kenya is in the middle of change. It's becoming more Westernized. Women, especially in the large cities like Nairobi, don't have to get married. Women can get divorced. Women can set up businesses. As runners, we are more accepted, recognized and supported."

The freedom of women to become athletes or something else of their choosing, of course, is not complete. There is much yet to be gained in Islamic countries, South America, India, and elsewhere. Still, global sports opportunities have aided in this evolving emancipation. It is a measure of success that women now compete in every Olympic event except boxing and wrestling, and that FIFA now counts women's soccer teams from 115 countries. The first World Cup for women took place only in 1991. These rapid changes have been enormously significant for the female half the world's population, and are reflective of the larger ongoing changes in world society.

## Technology, technique, and sports medicine

The application of technology to sports has also brought change for the athletes and for the public. Different training techniques, equipment, nutrition, and venues have improved performances. The idea of training and conditioning for an athletic event reaches back at least to the ancient Greeks, but the physical education techniques of Johan Friederich GutsMuths (1759–1839) and Friedrich Ludwig Jahn (1778–1852) in Germany led the way into the modern era of conditioning and gymnastics. The scientific revolution of the eighteenth and nineteenth centuries, in addition, brought continuing revelations of understanding. In 1893 Philippe Tissue carried out studies of fatigue in bicycle racers and at the same time the British philosopher Herbert Spencer began some of the first physiological research on muscular energy.

Sports medicine as a modern field of study began at the St Moritz Winter Olympics in 1928 when 33 physicians met to discuss the medical problems of athletes. Other practitioners, reaching far back into ancient history had been interested in therapeutic exercises and treatments, so this was not new except in an organizational sense. Periodic conferences, seminars, and academic journals such as the *Journal of Sports Medicine and Physical Fitness* (1961–), however, resulted from the initial organization and they were important for the exchange of information about the medical problems of athletes.

One of the more interesting nutritional advances had to do with dehydration. In somewhat whimsical manner this concern led to the invention of Gatorade, the first of the sports drinks now available for all people who exercise and sweat. At the University of Florida nephrologist Robert Cade became curious about a question asked by a research assistant and former football player. Why don't players urinate during practice? Cade and his assistants, thus, began to study the effects of dehydration and what could be done to replenish the body with the sodium, sugar, and water lost during heavy exercise. The lab technicians concocted a potion. When first served the drink during a 1965 game between the Florida Gators and the LSU Tigers a tackle exclaimed, "This tastes like piss," and poured the rest of the cup over his head.

As a thorough scientist Cade personally tested the player's assessment in his laboratory, tasted the potion, dismissed the accusation, and then improved the formula. Gatorade, now available in some 19 flavors dominates the sports-drink market with annual sales of over $2 billion. This successful sports elixir provides a $6 million yearly royalty payment to the university for the benefit of Cade's laboratory, 30 college scholarships, and an endowed chair for the faculty. Gatorade, in addition, improved the health of athletes.

Techniques also changed as athletes thought about their sports. At the 1952 Helsinki Olympics, for example, an unlikely Czechoslovakian, Emil Zatopek set records in the 5,000, 10,000, and marathon runs. He was scrawny, partly bald, and ran as if he would collapse at any moment. His face turned red, his head rolled back and forth, his arms flailed the air, and his tongue hung out. But he was fast enough to attract the communist Czechoslovakian government and he joined the army so that he could train. Using a flashlight and wearing army boots Zatopek worked out at night and developed a new conditioning regimen whereby he ran repeated high-speed 100-meter sprints interspersed with slow jogs. Today this is known as interval training and for Zatopek the technique made him nearly inexhaustible. He won the Olympic marathon even though he had never before run that distance, and as he chugged by with his unorthodox form the crowds chanted like a steam engine, "Za-to-pek! Za-to-pek! Za-to-pek!"

The USSR invaded Czechoslovakia in 1968 to suppress a liberal communist movement and Zatopek, saying that communism had to give the people "air to breathe", spoke out patriotically. As a result the government stripped "The Flying Czech" of his army rank and threw him out of the communist party. For over two decades the world lost sight of Zatopek as he tried to survive through 10 to 14 hours of manual labor per day. He was not allowed to travel and eventually obtained a job translating foreign sports journals at the Ministry of Sport. When the Cold War ended the government apologized for the abuse and restored his lost army rank. His invention of interval training, meanwhile, spread to other sports such as swimming and became an important part of conditioning routine.

Comparable also for changing the technique of a sport is the famous "Fosbury Flop" from the 1968 Mexico City Olympics. Dick Fosbury grew up as a gangly, awkward high school kid trying to be a high jumper using a scissors method whereby the jumper extends one leg over the bar followed by the other. He was unable to learn the popular straddle technique where the jumper rolls over the bar face down, and his scissors' attempts stalled at five feet six inches. At the point of preparing for a district championship in 1963 he got the idea of raising his hips and going over the bar lying backward, face up. He cleared five feet ten inches to the total shock of everyone. That was the beginning of the iconoclastic "flop."

Fosbury, leading more with his head and going over the bar with a backward arc, continued to refine his new technique despite the doubting coaches in high school and college. When he placed fifth in the NCAA championships his competitors who still used the straddle began to take notice. Fosbury became the most consistent seven-foot jumper in the nation and joined the Olympic team traveling to Mexico City. There he cleared seven foot four and a quarter inches, set the Olympic record, won gold, and demonstrated, as *Sports Illustrated* put it, "the Flop seen round the world." It changed the art of high jumping and floppers have dominated the event ever since that time.

Following the success of the sports schools in the Soviet Union and East Germany the USOC, belatedly, established a training center in the United States to teach and test the latest techniques. It was placed in Colorado Springs, Colorado, in 1977, at an abandoned Air Force Base and the USOC encouraged the national governing bodies to house their athletes and coaches on its campus for intensive and long-term training. A gymnasium, swimming flume, velodrome, track, sports medicine and biomechanics personnel, library, and dormitories provided the coaches and athletes with the best facilities for success. It was not only an effort to catch up with the communist sports factories, but also an application of science to sporting activity in the United States. It was as if the scientific and industrial revolutions of the eighteenth century, pioneered in the West, were at last being systematically applied to Western sports.

Out of the thrust of technology came new equipment. For swimmers there were tight Teflon-coated bodysuits that stretched from neck to knees to help ease the body through the water. It was, therefore, no longer necessary for swimmers to shave all the hair off their bodies to make them sleek in the pool. Archers who saw on high-speed cameras that their arrows traveled through the air like pieces of wriggling spaghetti began to use rigid arrows of aluminum and carbon with graphite coatings. Riflemen checked their shots with lasers, videotape, and heart monitors at the training center to uncover flaws in shooting technique. Runners began to wear special bodysuits to reduce wind resistance and ultra light-weight shoes with special spikes for the rubber tracks. Although bicycle regulations restricted innovations the cyclists adopted teardrop-shaped helmets, body-suits, and tires pumped to 250 pounds of pressure per square inch.

## Drugs and sports

The push to bring ongoing science and technology to bear on athletics, however, had a dark side—the utilization of illegal, performance-enhancing drugs. The drug problem became blatantly apparent at the 1976 Montreal Olympics where hefty female swimmers from East Germany won 11 of 13 races. When Shirley Babashoff, an American sprinter, suggested that their unusually deep voices resulted from male hormones an East German coach quipped, "They came to swim, not to sing." Indeed, Babashoff was right, but it was not proven at the time. With the collapse of the communist bloc in 1991 legal researchers found hidden in an East German military hospital a ten-volume archive that gave details about the drugs given to each athlete.

A teenage girl naturally produces half a milligram of testosterone, the main male hormone, per day. The communist sports doctors routinely pre-scribed up to 35 milligrams, 70 times the normal amount. In a male who naturally produces testosterone the effect was not so great, but in a young female the excessive testosterone produced heavy muscles, severe acne, a gruff voice, a growth of pubic hair across the abdomen, a soaring libido, and spectacular speed in the swimming pool.

Law suits against former coaches and doctors in the late 1990s exposed the process and the long-term damage of masculinized physiques, deep voices, deformed babies, liver dysfunction, internal bleeding, tumors, and depression. In the book *Faust's Gold* Steven Ungerleider related the testimony of Christiane Knacke-Sommer who began training under state supervision at age 13 and who won a bronze medal for East Germany at the 1980 Moscow Olympics. She was fed "little blue pills" and given injections that the coaches said were vitamins. She was never told that they were male hormones and when the prosecutor asked if she took them voluntarily she replied, "I was 15 years old when the pills started. The training motto at the pool was, 'You eat the pills, or you die.' It was forbidden to refuse."

She pointed at the defendants—coaches, doctors, and trainers at the trial—and exclaimed, "They destroyed my body and my mind. They gave me those pills, the Oral Turinablol, which made me crazy and ruined my body. They even poisoned my medal!" She stood up and threw her Olympic medal to the floor of the court chamber, "It is tainted, poisoned with drugs and a corrupt system. It is worthless and a terrible embarrassment to all Germans."

The drug problem that developed during the twentieth century was based upon scientific research that reached back into the nineteenth century. French physiologists theorized about "internal secretions," and eventually in 1935 German, Yugoslavian, and Dutch scientists produced synthetic testosterone to be used in medical therapy. Popular writer Paul de Kruif published information about this development in *The Male Hormone* (1945) and body builders began to take notice of the possibilities. Anabolic-androgenic steroids, the synthetic derivatives of testosterone, exaggerate secondary male sex characteristics, decrease body fat, and increase muscle bulk and strength. The steroids also heighten aggression. A swimmer told Ungerleider about the East German women, "They would look at you like they wanted to rip your tongue out." But the steroids did improve athletic performances by increasing strength and allowing quicker recovery from hard workouts.

Athletes have long searched for an "edge" in order to win. Outright bribery, of course, has existed in sports going back to the ancient Olympic games when Kallipos tried to buy off his opponents in the pentathlon. The judges fined his home city and when the Athenians refused to pay the Delphic oracle in turn refused to provide prophecies until the Athenians complied. The use of performance-enchancing drugs is not new either. Thomas Hicks of the United States, for example, collapsed after winning the marathon at the 1904 St Louis Olympics. Upon recovering he admitted that he had used strychnine and brandy during the run, and told reporters, "I would rather have won this race than be President of the United States." It was a bad omen.

Athletes have tried, among others things, vitamins, caffeine, oxygen, aspirin, Novocain, amphetamines, pregnancy, sexual abstinence, opium, alcohol, carbohydrate diets, and blood doping (reinfusion of an athlete's own stored blood). Seven US cyclists tried blood doping, or "boosting," at the 1984 Los Angeles Games to some advantage. Blood doping increases the amount of the red blood cells that carry oxygen, however, it is tricky because it can make the blood too thick, like sludge, and bring about a heart attack. The IOC banned blood doping in 1985. The East Germans once tried pumping air into swimmers' bowels to increase buoyancy. That did not work because it was too painful. The most disturbing technique to gain an edge, however, was the use of anabolic steroids and similar substances that altered the physique and physiology of the athlete. Such drugs, surely, violated the principle of fair play and altered natural human characteristics.

In 1952 the USSR at its first Olympic Games won seven medals in weight lifting. This was surprising and raised questions about the use of steroids. At the weightlifting championships in Vienna in 1954 Dr John Ziegler the team physician of the United States was able to obtain confirmation from a Soviet doctor during a tavern conversation. Ziegler came home to Maryland, tried some testosterone on himself, and then in 1958 administered dianabol, the first anabolic steroid, to three members of the east coast York Barbell Club. They soon reached world record levels, and the secret of the "little pink pills" leaked out to other athletes.

In 1971 US super-heavyweight lifter Ken Patera barely lost to USSR lifter Vasily Alexeyev and Patera looked forward to a rematch in the 1972 Olympic competition. "Last year, the only difference between me and him was that I couldn't afford his pharmacy bill," Patera told reporters. "Now I can. When I hit Munich next year I'll weigh in about 340, maybe 350. Then we'll see which are better—his steroids or mine." In the Olympic competition, however, Patera failed to clear his lifts and Alexeyev won. The IOC remained silent concerning his remarks.

The IOC, however, passed a resolution against performance-enhancing drugs in 1967, slowly began compiling a list of banned substances, and started trying to catch substance abusers at the 1968 Mexico City Games. Thus began the cat and mouse game that continues to the present. An unofficial poll of track and field athletes in the 1972 Olympics revealed a 68 percent steroid use. At the Commonwealth Games in 1974, 9 of 55 tests were positive; at the first Olympic testing for anabolic steroids in 1976 8 of 275 were guilty.

Following that exposure, substance users switched to black market exogenous testosterone and human growth hormone taken from the pituitary glands of cadavers. When an unofficial screening at the 1980 Moscow Olympics revealed that 20 percent of the participants used testosterone, the IOC banned it. At the 1983 Caracas Pan American Games sophisticated urine tests surprised the participants and officials caught 15 athletes from 10 countries. Following the initial disqualifications 11 Americans quickly withdrew from the competition and flew home. Weightlifter Jeff Michels who failed the tests said, "We were told steroids is the only thing they look for."

To avoid detection athletes tried going off illegal drugs a few weeks before competition, flushing themselves with a diuretic, and sometimes trying to substitute someone else's urine for the test. Cagey testers learned to watch as the sample was taken so some athletes injected clean urine into their bladder with a catheter before a test. This did not work well and was painful. A bizarre situation occurred when Martti Vainio of Finland failed a steroid test and lost his silver medal for the 10,000-meter run in the 1984 Olympics. He had given up steroids months before the competition, but had used blood boosting with his own stored blood. The steroids were in the stored blood that he injected before the race and he was caught. The best solution for cheaters, however, was to use a "designer drug" that would mask the use of steroids, or one that the tests could not detect.

It is an irony that the Canadian sprinter Ben Johnson was caught and disqualified in the 1988 Seoul Olympics. Charlie Frances, Johnson's coach, recommended a cycle of drugs including various steroids and human growth hormone to his athletes. Johnson used a diuretic to flush his system shortly before competition and should have been clean. However, stanozolol, an anabolic steroid that Francis thought he did not use was detected in his system.

There had been earlier allegations about Johnson's drug use due to his extreme muscle definition, marked improvement of performance in a short period of time, and yellowed eyes, a sign of liver dysfunction. He had not been caught, however, and there might even have been an error in the testing that turned up the stanozolol. He may not have been guilty for that particular drug, but he was surely guilty about the general use of drugs. Johnson, stripped of his medal, returned home to Canada in disgrace. Concerning the use of drugs by athletes Charlie Francis argued, "I don't call it cheating. My definition of cheating is doing something nobody else is doing." Sadly, after a two-year suspension Johnson was caught again and banned from track competition for life.

For three years, 1986–1989, a doctor and two coaches from East Germany visited China to help set up a drug program with the result that Chinese weightlifters, swimmers, and runners began to perform superhuman feats. At the 1988 world weightlifting championship the Chinese women came from nowhere and won nine of nine divisions. Chinese women ran the four fastest marathons of the year in 1993, and five women runners surpassed world records in ten events at a national championship in Beijing in 1993. Wang Junxia clipped 42 seconds off the 10,000-meter record and 16 seconds from the 3,000-meter mark. Qu Yunxia broke the 1,500-meter record by almost two seconds. Since world records are usually lowered by small increments there was an immediate suspicion of drug usage, but the coach, Ma Junren, attributed the achievements to hard training and the use of traditional Chinese supplements such as turtle blood and caterpillar fungus.

Chinese swimmers won 3 silver medals and 1 bronze medal at the 1988 Seoul Olympics; they won 4 gold and 5 silver medals at the 1992 Barcelona Olympics; and they won 12 of the 16 events at the world swimming championships in Rome in September 1994. In October 1994, however, 3 of the women and 4 of the men swimmers tested positive for dehydrotestosterone, a banned substance. At the Asian Games in 1994 7 of 17 tested swimmers turned up positive and the others revealed high elevations for steroids. It was the East German system all over again. China had created another athletic machine complete with screening youngsters for athletic talent, special sports schools, and anabolic steroids. While the Soviet Union had had 46 sports boarding schools and East Germany had 20, the Chinese had 150.

The IOC which became dimly cognizant of the drug problem in 1967 remained reactive rather than proactive in its testing procedures. It conducted exams during an Olympic competition, but depended upon national committees and athletic federations to police athletes at other times. The USOC, for example, first began to test at national championships in 1978, started mandatory checks outside of competition with a 48-hour notice in 1992, and started to test outside of competition with no warning in 1996. Dr. Robert Voy, the director of testing for the USOC in 1984 and 1988 commented,

> Athletes are a walking laboratory, and the Olympics have become a proving ground for scientists, chemists, and unethical doctors. The testers know that the [illegal drug] gurus are smarter than they are. They know how to get in under the radar.

At the 1996 Atlanta Games the IOC examined 2,000 out of 11,000 athletes and found two positive tests. They discovered Russian athletes using a new drug, bromantan, that aided the recovery from exercise, but it was too new and the IOC issued no sanctions. Urine tests also did not catch human growth hormone and among the athletes the "clean" Atlanta Games were jokingly called the Growth Hormone Games.

The crisis about drugs deepened: in 1997–1998 the Australian Olympic Committee turned up 3,200 positive cases among their athletes; at the 1998 world championships in Australia a Chinese swimmer was found with 13 vials of human growth hormone in her luggage; at the Tour de France in 1998 the Italian team, Festina, was expelled after erythropoietin (EPO), a drug that stimulates red blood cell production, was found in their masseur's car; en route to breaking the major league baseball home run record Mark McGwire unabashedly admitted using the steroid, androstenedione. Under pressure, the IOC called a conference at Lausanne, Switzerland and created the semi-independent World Anti-Doping Agency (WADA) that began operation on 13 January 2000. It was dedicated to year-round, out-of-competition testing, education, and research to develop better exams. The cat and mouse game, however, continued.

On 13 June 2003 a test tube of clear liquid from a syringe arrived by mail at the Olympic drug laboratory at the University of California from WADA. A track coach had turned it in and said it contained an unknown anabolic steroid used by athletes. After three months of work Dr Donald H. Catlin and his chemists found tetrahydrogestrinone (THG) and developed a test to catch the people who used it. The anonymous tipster also identified the source of the designer drug and court investigations commenced. The case, still incomplete late in 2003, apparently involves a number of world-class athletes in Olympic competition as well as in professional competition from a variety of sports. Catlin commented: "I'm interested to see how sport responds. If it takes a deep hard look at this, there could be fundamental changes. I don't want to be finding another big bust in five years. I'm fearful of that."

What Catlin fears, of course, is already in the laboratory. At the University of Pennsylvania's Department of Physiology in 1999 Dr. H. Lee Sweeney led a team of researchers to examine the effects of injecting a synthetic gene into the muscles of a mouse to continuously stimulate muscle growth. The mouse grew 60 percent more muscle than normal and with that single treatment maintained the muscles without diminution into old age. Because of the Human Genome Project that mapped the 100,000 genes of human DNA synthetic genes are now becoming available to alter human potential. It will be possible in the near future to expand muscles, increase the red cell count, enlarge the size of blood vessels, and repair torn tendons. Biotechnology has enormous medical potential, but already several weightlifters have contacted Sweeney to obtain an injection. As Sweeney related, "Safety data didn't mean anything to them. They basically said they were willing to do it right now. I told them the FDA wouldn't be fine with that and I could go to jail if I helped them."

The technique of implanting genes to change muscle function, however, is not difficult and growth hormone releasing hormone (GHRH) which can be detected only with a biopsy will likely be the next big problem. Genetic manipulation is already over the horizon and it raises a fundamental problem for everyone. Norwegian speed skater and Olympic gold medallist Johann Olav Koss who is a physician and an athlete's representative to the IOC commented,

> This is an ethical question, not only for sport, but for the human race. You are tinkering with nature. How far are you going to go? . . . Why shouldn't we create something genetically that is much smarter, stronger and better than a human? Why shouldn't we put wings on a

human? Why shouldn't we give humans the eyes of a fly? Then we are no longer human, we are something else.

The athletic apocalypse is upon us. "Clean" athletes are defeated and ridiculed. Swimmer Shirley Babashoff who complained about the East German girls in 1976 was called "Surly Shirley," and the US coach was labeled a failure. He was never offered an Olympic coaching position again. Harm to the health of the athlete has been proven, and no one can ever be certain of fair competition.

With the revelation in 2003 that 5–7 percent of major league baseball players turned up positive for steroids after being warned that they would be tested, Dave Kindred of *Sporting News* wrote,

> Great damage has been done. It's damage that won't be repaired for years . . . This is a systemic failure that has created, in essence, a breach of contract with fans who pony up good money to see games contested on a level playing field. Now every player is suspect, every base hit suspect, every strikeout. In a game that defines its essential fairness and timeless beauty by statistics and sanctifies players according to their numbers, what now? Does 73 [the homerun record] mean anything now? What to do with a man who three times in four seasons hit more homeruns than Babe Ruth's 60?

Cynicism has been the result, and it smears even the "clean" athlete who presents a performance that people should applaud as an example of human ability and spirit. Instead, great performances are questioned.

The drug culture unfortunately has seeped into all levels of sport. Bob Goldman, a Chicago physician and author, asked 198 athletes in 1995 if they would take a banned drug if they were guaranteed to win and not be caught. All but three said, "Yes." Goldman then followed with a second hypothetical situation. Would they take a performance-enhancing substance if they would not be caught, win every event they entered in the next five years, and then die from the side effects? More than half said, "Yes." This poll raises questions about the motivation of the athlete.

The venerable answer, of course, is that the athlete strives for the glory, prestige, and self-satisfaction of being the best. It was expressed by the gesture of victory observed by Bernd Heinrich in the stone-age drawings of Africa. Another answer about the motivation is that winning athletes have also been rewarded with tangible goods, such as the pots of olive oil given to ancient Greek Olympians. At the present time, successful athletes, however, are rewarded with money. The fabulous contracts given in the professional leagues and the prizes for winning, or even competing, in other world-class events provide a powerful incentive. This is due to the commodification of sport, that is, turning sport into a business commodity that can be bought and sold.

## The commercialization of sport

The early modern sports promoters of boxing and horseracing, and later ones of baseball, football, and soccer learned readily that people would pay to see a performance. Team owners thus built stadiums where they could charge admission, advertise, and pay outstanding athletes. Cities and nations, meanwhile, constructed a technical infrastructure that supported the economy and, incidentally, the commercialization of sports. Railroads and telegraph wires provided an initial spider web of communications in the nineteenth century. This was followed by telephones, motion pictures, radios, airplanes, and televisions. The infrastructure allowed for competition by athletes between cities and nations, and for fans to keep track of the action.

Newspapers and sports papers first brought sports reports to a curious public—*The American Turf Register and Sporting Magazine* (1829), *Spirit of the Times and Life in New York* (1831), *Sporting Life* (1883), *Sporting News* (1886) in the United States; *Sporting Magazine* (1792), *Sporting Life* (1821), *Athletic News* (1875), *Scottish Athletic Journal* (1882) in Britain; *Le Sport* (1854) in France. There were scattered sports reports in the major newspapers, but when Joseph Pulitzer bought the *New York Herald* in 1882 he set up a sports department. Sports columns appeared before World War I and sports journalists such as Ring Lardner began to receive bylines.

Radio sportscasters, such as Graham McNamee and Bill Stern, provided eyewitness accounts to remote fans starting in the 1920s. Until this point it was mainly the people in the stands that provided the income for the promoters, although there might be money to be made from a reproduction of the event on film. George L. "Tex" Rickard, the first professional fight promoter, for example, filmed the heavyweight bout between Jack Johnson and James Jeffries in 1910. Profit from the film, however, was limited by a nationwide fit of racism that censored its showing.

Radio companies uncovered the profitability of selling "commercials" or sponsorships to businesses wanting to advertise their goods to a broad, unseen market. Interestingly enough, companies discovered that people would buy the products advertised on their favorite radio show, and athletes discovered that people would buy the products that they endorsed. Thus, radio helped to forge a commercial link with sports that continues, albeit with greater sophistication, to the present time.

Bill Stern announced the first televised sporting event in the United States from New York City—a baseball game between Princeton and Columbia universities in May 1939. Although there were only 400 receiving sets in the city the baseball game was followed by a bicycle race and boxing match. In the fall the Mutual Broadcasting System paid $2,500 to the National Football League for the right to show its championship game and broadcast commercials. This faltering start demonstrated the potential for sports entertainment, but the development had to wait for the end of World War II.

In 1950 about 9 percent of Americans owned a television set. In 1955 the figure was 65 percent, and in 1965 ownership was 93 percent. The same dramatic acquisition held true in Great Britain. The use of color sets in 1970 was 39 percent; in 1972 it was 64 percent. Globally, the number of television sets per 100 people reached 23.4 in 1997. Networks aimed their sports broadcasts at male weekend fans and improved the presentation to give the viewer a feel for being at the stadium.

Roone Arledge (1931–2002) the director of ABC sports ordered cameras placed in blimps and on cranes for multiple views; used close-up shots of athletes and coaches; pointed microphones at the sound of the action and the roar of the crowd; provided pictures of the fans and cheerleaders; pioneered instant replay; and employed experts to not only describe the action, but also to explain it as well. He began *Wide World of Sports* (1961–1998) and wrote the famous lines repeated at the introduction of every show, "Spanning the globe to bring you the constant variety of sport, the thrill of victory, the agony of defeat, the human drama of athletic competition." In 1968 ABC became the first network to televise the Olympic Games. They repeated their coverage in 1972 and 1976. Above all others Arledge popularized sports television and gave it an international dimension.

Television became a revolutionizing medium for sports. Since it was time-bound in its scheduling and advertising, sports such as tennis that have no certain ending if the score is tied, had to be circumscribed with quick tie-breaking rules to determine a winner and end play. Colleges and professional teams scrambled their schedules, traditions, and rules in order to fit into television time slots. In return, television provided an enormous amount of money. In 1964 CBS paid $14 million for the right to televise professional football and in 1985 each team received $65 million from a television package. Currently, the NFL holds an eight-year contract with four networks for $17.6 billion. In 1977 the NCAA signed a four-year contract with ABC for $120 million and in 1981 agreed with ABC, CBS, and Turner Broadcasting for a price of $74.3 million per year. FIFA sold its rights for soccer championships in 1990, 1994, and 1998 for $78 million each showing. TV sports contracts from 1990 to 1994 in the United States amounted to $3.6 billion and the amount charged for commercials spiraled upward. When Arledge and ABC started Monday Night Football in 1970 they charged $65,000 per minute; in 1982 they charged $185,000 for half a minute. Currently, the cost for a Super Bowl ad is $75,000 per second.

The amount of money paid to professional athletes likewise soared. The average salary for a major league baseball player reached $2 million in 2001. It was $420,000 in 1988. The average salary for a National Football League player jumped from $660,000 to $1,170,000 per year from 1993 to 2000. The highest paid, Drew Bledsoe who was quarterback for the New England Patriots received $8.5 million per year in 2000. Troy Aikman, another quarterback, held a contract with the Dallas Cowboys worth $85.5 million for the years 1997–2007. Shaquille O'Neal, a basketball player for the Los Angeles Lakers played for $120 million for the years 1997–2003. David Beckham, perhaps the most famous contemporary soccer player, received $8.8 million per year from Manchester United. The richest contract of all, however, went to Alex Rodriguez with a baseball agreement of $252 million for 2001–2010.

Television capabilities improved. Australia received live broadcasts of the 1956 Melbourne Games, but the rest of the world was left out. European viewers saw the current events of the 1960 Rome Olympics which were then relayed to Japan, the United States, and Canada. The first live coverage via satellite came with the 1964 Tokyo Games. In 1974 direct broadcast satellites, the first communications satellites, allowed the relay of television into targeted areas where the signal could be received by a dish and sent out over a cable. In the 1980s fiber optics that would not wear out nor show the effect of moisture or heat replaced copper wires. Silicon lines the size of a human hair carried dozens of programs at once, and with digital compression a TV set could receive as many as 500 channels. A British company established the first global digital optical system in 1991.

The technological advances gave opportunity to media barons such as Ted Turner and Rupert Murdoch who saw the world as a rich marketplace. Turner (1938–) created in 1980 the international news channel, CNN, that reached 143 nations by 1993; purchased the Atlanta Braves baseball team; and sponsored the Goodwill Games (1986–2001) between the United States and the Soviet Union. Murdoch (1931–) built upon his father's newspaper business in Australia, procured papers in the United States including the *New York Post*; purchased Twentieth Century Fox in the 1980s; started Fox News Channel in 1996; and bought sports teams in Australia, Germany, Britain, and the United States. He established satellite networks in Asia and Europe, and announced to his BskyB satellite shareholders in 1996, "We intend to use sports as a battering ram and a lead offering in all our pay television offerings."

Sports equipment companies also became international corporations. Philip Knight and Bill Bowerman, for example, started Nike in the 1960s and used an unwritten "Swoosh" logo so that it could be universally recognized. Knight followed cheap labor and manufactured his equipment, often through subcontractors, in Japan in the 1970s, Korea in the 1980s, and Southeast Asia in the 1990s. Criticized for such labor actions—a South Korean girl earned 15 cents per hour to make shoes that cost $5.60 in Korea and sold for $70 in the United States—Nike merely shrugged that they had created jobs where none existed before. Nike along with Reebok, Adidas, and Converse competed by supplying athletes and teams with their equipment in hope of promoting sales. Nike became a multinational company with most of its products manufactured abroad and more than half of its sales in foreign markets. The company controlled about one-third of the global market for sports equipment in the mid-1990s when Knight pronounced, "Sports has become the dominant entertainment of the world."

Like others, Nike used superstar athletes to advertise its products and its foremost salesman was Michael Jordan (1963–). He was born in Brooklyn, played 12 professional basketball seasons with the Chicago Bulls, and later became a player-owner with the Washington Wizards. He was a member of the gold medal "Dream Team" of the 1992 Barcelona Olympics, and generally is considered one of the greatest basketball players of all time. Jordan, in addition, was hard working, non-controversial, handsome, likable, a role model, and thus ideal for advertisements. He made $30 million a year with the Bulls and twice that amount with his endorsements. He represented Chevrolet, McDonald's, Coca-Cola, Johnson Products, and Nike. The Nike Air Jordan shoe became the world's most profitable sports shoe.

To the approval of his sponsors Jordan was discreet. He made no political statements, did not use drugs, tried to stay outside the Asian labor controversies of Nike, and when he had to wear Reebok clothing at Barcelona he casually draped a US flag over the Reebok logo while on the victory stand. In 1997 during exhibition games in Paris a reporter asked Jordan if he were a god. To his credit the superstar replied, "I play a game of basketball. I try to entertain for two hours and then let people go home to their lives . . . I could never consider myself a god." Jordan thus became an exemplar for the new global sports capitalism. He was a great basketball player and also a sports commodity magnified through the advertisements of his sponsors.

## The Olympics and commercialization

A singular case study of the global commercialization of sport involves the Olympic Games and its five-ring logo. Baron de Coubertin designed the logo, the blue, black, red, yellow, and green interlocked rings, and began using it on his stationery in 1913. At a conference in 1914 the rings were first used on an Olympic flag. In 1928 Coca-Cola began to participate by providing a training table. The IOC did not like the commercialism, but needed the money. A Los Angeles baker, Paul Helms, produced Olympic bread for the 1932 Los Angeles Games, but patriotically gave up his legal right to the name to the USOC. The US Congress incorporated the USOC in 1950 and gave it control over the motto, name, and logo. It was at this point that the poorly funded USOC began to sniff the commercial value of Olympic fame.

When he became president of the IOC in the early 1950s Avery Brundage saw the money potential of television and opened discussions with his colleagues. His idea was that the IOC should control the television contracts and share the money with the local groups and sports federations. He eventually brokered an agreement in 1966 that one-third of the television money would go to the IOC for sharing and two-thirds would go to the local organizing committee that hosted the games. Before this the IOC had no income—rich men ran the IOC and Brundage, himself, paid his own expenses. This new arrangement opened a pandora's box of conflicts and friction since it was the local committees that negotiated the TV contracts and wanted the money. In 1977 the IOC insisted upon joining the negotiations and began to release the use of the Olympic name for a 30 percent share in the profit of the sale of licensed items.

There was a crisis, however, with the 1984 Los Angeles Games. The 1976 Montreal Games cost about $2 billion and had left the city and province struggling with crushing debt. The Moscow Games suffered a boycott and then it was the turn of Los Angeles. No other city had bid for the games because of the Montreal financial disaster and the anxious people of Los Angeles hastily amended their charter to prevent the use of public money for the games.

Peter Ueberroth the president of the Los Angeles Olympic Organizing Committee (LAOOC), consequently, relied upon private funding. He ignored the IOC and personally negotiated television contracts in the United States, Europe, Australia and Asia totaling $286 million. He limited the sponsors so that there would be no product overlap and required a minimum $4 million contribution. Kodak dallied and so Ueberroth gave the film sponsorship to Fuji which then promptly increased its market share in the US from 3 to 9 percent. Ueberroth sold off kilometers of the torch relay for youth charities. He used existing facilities for the athletic events whenever possible and the visiting athletes lived in college dormitories.

Ueberroth started with a cardboard box left over from the 1932 Los Angeles Games and made a profit of $215 million. "But from the beginning I said, doom sayers be damned," he commented:

> The Olympics were the perfect vehicle to join the public and private sectors in a partnership. It had all the right elements: youth, healthy competition, tradition, drama, and a worldwide audience. It was an

opportunity for private enterprise to enhance itself and show what is good about mankind.

The IOC received a reduced amount of the largess, but the "Private Enterprise Olympics" was a chauvinistic US success that encouraged other cities to bid for future Olympiads.

The IOC continued its business of sports and under "The Olympic Program" (TOP) in 1985 began to market its logo in host cities for a 3 percent fee, later changed to 5 percent. The five-rings, consequently, along with the Nike "Swoosh" became the most recognized non-written symbol in the world. The IOC negotiated a television contract with NBC of $2.3 billion for summer and winter games in 2004, 2006, and 2008. The USOC would get 12.75 percent of this amount. All was not fun and profit, however.

The Olympic officials have been accused of covering up drug usage in order to protect the business relations with sponsors, and for the 2002 Salt Lake City Winter Games the IOC had to endure a scandal involving bribes for site votes. In one egregious instance the representative from Cameroon was promised a college scholarship for his daughter in exchange for his vote to award the Olympics to Salt Lake City. The scandal led to the resignation of four IOC members, six expulsions, and ten warnings. The local Salt Lake leaders escaped prosecution, but now the IOC must send inspection teams at its own expense without the generosity of a potential host city. Robert K. Barney, Stephen R. Wenn, and Scott G. Martyn, the Canadian writers of *Selling the Five Rings* (2002) conclude their discussion about the commodification of the Olympics by asking the question, "Who are the games for?"

Once the television money became available it was not too surprising that the IOC evolved into an international business organization that had no boundaries. It was beholden to the inhibiting laws of no nation. Coubertin and the founders of the Olympic movement had worried about the corrupting influence of money and therefore embraced amateurism. The ideal of amateurism, however, died and the IOC became wealthy. It now has business motives and works for its own survival through the commercialization of its sports activities.

Peter Pocklington, the owner of the Edmonton Oilers hockey team, had a phrase for this modern business evolution of sports. In 1988 he sold Canada's greatest player, Wayne Gretsky, to the Los Angeles Kings despite the outrage of hometown fans. Pocklington explained that Gretsky's contract would run out in four years and at that point the contract would be worth nothing to the Oilers. So, Gretsky was sold while his contract still had value. For the owner it was a rational decision. "Sports is too much of a business to be a sport," Pocklington advised.

## Sports venues

Since the Olympics shifted sites every four years there was opportunity for cities to build new venues of high quality to enhance the commercialization. Swimming pools, for example, became deeper and wider with wave-absorbing gutters and lane ropes that ensured smooth water for competition. Diving wells for platform and springboard performers were made deeper for safety and equipped with bubbling devices that ruffled the top of the water so that a twisting, somersaulting diver could see the otherwise transparent surface. Rubber composition tracks started to replace dirt and cinder tracks in the 1960s and in 1961 the first widespread use of artificial snow machines began in the United States ski resorts.

This was part of a long-time attempt to neutralize the interference of the physical environment; the thought of improving a venue for players was nothing new. Baseball, cricket, soccer, and American football fields as well as golf courses had been rolled, cut, and manicured since the nineteenth century. In 1965, however, the outer limit was achieved when technology provided an example of complete control over nature with the opening of the Astrodome. It was a triumph that some purists did not like, but it so challenged the concept of a stadium that no spectator, athlete, or city could ever forget it. It was also reflective of stadium extravagance that only a wealthy society could afford.

Since 79 CE the model for a stadium had been the ancient Roman Colesseum—open air, multileveled, a flexible arena space for athletic presentations, and massive seating. Until 1965 most stadiums followed that pattern, but it was a millionaire judge from Houston, Texas who saw something different. As a tourist, Roy M. Hofheinz visited Rome and heard the story of the Colesseum and noted that the Roman engineers tried to cool the stadium with the chill air from fountains and with the shade of awnings that reached at least part way over the top.

Hofheinz and a group of millionaire investors had acquired a major league baseball franchise in 1960 and had promised to build a new stadium for the team. The summer climate in Houston was beastly with the temperature and humidity both usually registering in the high ranges. The suffocating climate provided no relief at night, and in addition, the surrounding coastal land supplied inexhaustible armies of mosquitoes. Hofheinz figured, "If those Romans could put a lid on their stadium, so can we," and therefore he proposed an air-conditioned stadium large enough to encompass a baseball field.

He consulted engineers who told him that it was feasible, but had never been done. A design firm constructed a model and Hofheinz proceeded to sell the idea to Houston businessmen and area voters who approved the tax bonds to finance the project. Constructed away from the downtown home of the Houston Astros baseball team, the Astrodome opened in 1965 at a cost of $45 million. The roof was a flat, elongated arch with a clear span of 642 feet that was 218 feet above the playing field. It was dotted with closely spaced skylights to let in sunlight and held up by a latticework of black steel trusses. Inside there were six colored tiers of cushioned seats with no obstructed view and all positioned to look toward second base. At the top was a ring of blue skyboxes where large groups could enjoy television, lounge chairs, and private kitchen facilities. The inside temperature was 72°F and the powerful air-conditioning system easily exhausted the cigarette smoke of the fans.

Perhaps most impressive was the huge 474-foot scoreboard that could flash commercials, lead cheers, and keep the score. When an Astro hit a home run the scoreboard set off rockets, blew whistles, and featured a cowboy shooting bullets that would ricochet from one side of the scoreboard to the other. The Astrodome could seat 45,000 fans for baseball and 52,000 for football, but it was a multiuse stadium that hosted conventions, circuses, trade shows, and a variety of other sports.

The day before the opening game the Astro players discovered a terrible design flaw. The fielders could not track fly balls as they arced across the glaring backlight of the sunlit dome and the players had to wear protective batting helmets as the balls dropped around them. After several days of panic the solution of painting the skylights solved the problem. Then, however, the grass died and the Astrodome threatened to become an indoor dust bowl. Hofheinz, however, ingeniously installed a carpet of experimental artificial grass invented by Chemstrand that subsequently became known as AstroTurf.

AstroTurf, the first artificial surface for field sports, was cheap to maintain and later used for both indoor and outdoor athletic fields. In the face of complaints about abrasions and injuries, however, competing versions of the artificial surface began to use combinations of live grass and synthetic blades, or different weaves of synthetic fibers along with various combinations of subsurface pads. The Astrodome is now obsolete and the city built the enormous Reliant Stadium with a retractable roof next door. Nonetheless, it was the Astrodome that first offered air-conditioning, comfortable seating, skyboxes, the huge scoreboard, and an artificial playing surface. This was a facility that completely controlled the environment and offered pure baseball—no wind, no distracting light, no rain, no mud, no bumps in the playing surface. Other cities subsequently built their own version of the Astrodome—New Orleans, Seattle, Indianapolis, Pontiac, St Petersburg, San Antonio.

Some critics complained about the loss of the vagaries of weather and a wave of nostalgia for old stadiums in the 1990s brought about a compromise with contemporary stadiums that have sliding roofs that can be closed for inclement weather—Houston, Phoenix, Toronto, Seattle, Milwaukee. Perhaps the most innovative stadium at present, however, is the Gelredome in Arnhem, Netherlands. This stadium for 26,000 fans has a retractable roof of solar panels to provide energy for heating or air-conditioning, and also a sliding soccer field installed upon a huge concrete foundation. When not in use the grass field is trundled out of the stadium into the sunlight for healthy turf. This solves the problem of the poor grass growth in retractable roof stadiums, and at the same time leaves available a large venue for concerts or exhibitions.

The criticism about the new stadiums reaches beyond the technology into the commercial and social realm. The stadiums of the early twentieth century were built within easy access by fans, but starting with the Astrodome the stadiums moved to be near suburban highway systems. This tended to preclude any sort of community feeling for the team. Sportswriter John Eisenberg commented, for example,

> At the Cotton Bowl [in Dallas] the Cowboys had been a working man's team on rollicking, emotional, and slightly naughty Sundays. At Texas Stadium [in Irving between Dallas and Fort Worth], they took on a regal bearing as a showpiece of what amounted to a social club. Home games were no longer emotional outpourings; they were social occasions.

The movement of teams, the trading of players, and the threats of team owners to move unless they obtained new stadiums at public expense has further damaged feelings of loyalty. Mayor Bob Lanier of Houston dealing with threats from the Oilers football team said, "Can you ask the average guy to build luxury suites for rich people, so they can support rich owners, so they can pay rich players?" There exists little proof that a new stadium helps the economy of a city; the value seems psychic. How inhabitants feel about their hometown and the pleasure people derive from following "their" team—unmeasurable factors—are most important for the support of stadiums and athletic programs. These are the basic reasons why citizens agree to tax themselves for sports and in Houston the people eventually paid for both a new baseball and a new football stadium.

## Sports and the future

Professional sports have always had to be businesslike in order to survive and to pay the athletes. Now however, the IOC, once the citadel of sports for the love of sports, operates on a profit basis with champions who are awarded by their home nations. This is not much different than the situation of the ancient Olympics where the participants evolved into professionals and were rewarded by their city-states. Add to this circumstance, however, the pervasive performance-enhancing drug culture and the ideal of modern sports whereby people compete under equal conditions is shattered. Who can tell if the local high school fullback or track star is taking human growth hormone? Doesn't that reduce the expectant uncertainty of outcome that all sports have in common? What about the hovering specter of human genetic engineering that might produce athletic monsters? Will records mean anything anymore? Is this the picture of postmodern sports? Who cares?

Yet, there are many "clean" athletes and people who want equality in competition. The IOC and various sports organizations have taken a stand against the drug culture. Perhaps, they will win the cat and mouse game, and the natural artistry of athletes on an international or local level will continue to take the real measure of human limitations. Moreover, flickering samples of sportsmanship endure. At the Olympic taekwondo trials in 2000, for example, the number-one ranked US woman, Kay Poe, dislocated her knee in a preliminary match. She could stand only on one leg for the final encounter to win an Olympic berth. At the match the number-two ranked fighter, friend Esther Kim, simply bowed down to her at the beginning and surrendered the bout. Kim thought, "This is the first time in my life I really feel like a champion." Beyond such moments of self-sacrificing fairness, the individual "sheer joy" of human movement felt by Roger Bannister as he ran along a beach in his youth will remain always an inborn part of every human being. Therein lies the hope for global sports and sports at all levels.

## Further reading

Michael Bamberger and Don Yeager, "Over the Edge," *Sports Illustrated*, vol. 86 (April 14, 1997), pp. 62–70; Robert K. Barney, Stephen R. Wenn, and Scott G. Martyn, *Selling the Five Rings* (Salt Lake City: University of Utah Press, 2002); Susan Brownell, *Training the Body for China* (Chicago: University of Chicago, 1995); John Eisenberg in Brad Schultz, "A Geographical Study of the American Ballpark," *International Journal of the History of Sport*, vol. 20 (March 2003), pp. 127–142; Allen Guttmann, *Women's Sports* (New York: Columbia, 1991); Christopher R. Hill, *Olympic Politics* (Manchester: Manchester University Press, 1992); Dave Kindred, "A shot in the arm baseball didn't need," *Sporting News*, vol. 227 (November 24, 2003), p. 68; Raymond Krise and Bill Squires, *Fast Tracks: the History of Distance Running* (Brattleboro, Vermont: Stephen Greene Press, 1982); Walter LaFeber, *Michael Jordan and the New Global Capitalism* (New York: Norton, 2001); Jim Riordan, "The Rise, Fall and Rebirth of Sporting Women in Russia and the USSR," *Journal of Sport History*, vol. 18 (Spring 1991), pp. 183–199; Randy Roberts and James S. Olson, *Winning is the Only*

*Thing* (Baltimore, Maryland: Johns Hopkins, 1989); Paul D. Staudohar and James A. Mangan, *The Business of Professional Sports* (Urbana, Illinois: University of Illinois, 1991); E. M. Swift and Don Yeager, "Unnatural Selection," *Sports Illustrated*, vol. 94 (May 14, 2001), pp. 88–94; Terry Todd, "Anabolic Steroids: The Gremlins of Sport," *Journal of Sport History*, vol. 14 (Spring 1987), pp. 87–107; Peter Ueberroth in Christopher R. Hill, *Olympic Politics* (Manchester: Manchester University Press, 1992), p. 161; Steven Ungerleider, *Faust's Gold* (New York: St Martins, 2001); Hans Westerbeek and Aaron Smith, *Sport Business in the Global Marketplace* (New York: Palgrave, 2003); Wayne Wilson and Edward Derse (eds), *Doping in Elite Sports* (Champaign, Illinois: Human Kinetics, 2001).

# Index